Excuse me, please...

Englisch für touristische Alltagssituationen

ELISABETH STRÖM

VERITAS

Die Deutsche Bibliothek – CIP-Einheitsaufnahme

Ström, Elisabeth:
Excuse me, please : Englisch für touristische
Alltagssituationen / Elisabeth Ström. – Linz : Veritas, 2000
(MUMMM)
ISBN 3-7058-5557-3

Wir haben versucht, die Texte im vorliegenden Band geschlechtergerecht zu formulieren.
Um aber die Lesbarkeit nicht zu beeinträchtigen, haben wir uns dazu entschlossen, nur Formen wie „SchülerIn" oder „LehrerIn" statt „Schülerin oder Schüler" bzw. „Lehrerin oder Lehrer" zu verwenden und in der Folge auch Artikel, Pronomen und Adjektive lediglich in der weiblichen Form anzuführen.
Dass selbstverständlich auch Männer angesprochen sein sollen, das soll das große I im Wortinneren, das auch in den Pluralformen verwendet wird, verdeutlichen. Wir bitten um Verständnis.

© 1997 Elisabeth Ström and Bokforlaget Natur och Kultur, Stockholm
Deutsche Lizenzausgabe: VERITAS-VERLAG, Linz
Alle Rechte, insbesondere das Recht der Verbreitung, auch durch Film, Fernsehen, fotomechanische Wiedergabe,
Bild- und Tonträger jeder Art, oder auszugsweiser Nachdruck, vorbehalten
1. Auflage (2000)
Gedruckt in Österreich auf umweltfreundlich hergestelltem Papier
Übersetzung: Waltraud Jungreithmayr, Gunskirchen
Lektorat: Andreas Schneider, Lenzing
Umschlaggestaltung: Germana Kolmhofer, Hartkirchen
Illustrationen S. 19, 91: Annika Frostell
Umschlagillustrationen: Margit Feyrer-Fleischhanderl, Linz
Satz: GraphicWorks, Grieskirchen
Druck, Bindung: Friedrich VDV, Linz

ISBN 3-7058-5557-3

Vorwort

„*Excuse me, please …*" ist ein Lehrmittel für Kommunikation und Konversation im Englischunterricht, das Ihnen die Arbeit im mündlichen Bereich des Englischunterrichts wesentlich erleichtern soll. Das Übungsmaterial regt Schüler dazu an, ihre Englischkenntnisse in Alltagssituationen praxisbezogen anzuwenden. Es besteht aus Kopiervorlagen, die in acht verschiedene Alltagsbereiche unterteilt sind. Dabei kann die ganze Klasse gemeinsam an einem Thema arbeiten; es können aber auch einzelne Gruppen verschiedene Themen behandeln. Da das Material nicht an ein bestimmtes Niveau oder Lehrbuch gebunden ist, kann es völlig frei eingesetzt werden.

Einsatzmöglichkeiten von „*Excuse me, please …*":
- als Ergänzung zum Lehrbuch in der Hauptschule, in der AHS und in berufsbildenden Schulen;
- in der Erwachsenenbildung;
- als Unterrichtsmittel für spezielle Themenbereiche, Wahlfächer;
- als Vorbereitung für Schul-, Arbeits- oder Urlaubsaufenthalte im Ausland.

Die Sprache basiert auf britischem Englisch. In einigen Fällen wurden amerikanische Wörter und Ausdrücke parallel zu den britischen verwendet; in diesem Fall sind die Varianten mit (*BrE*) für britisches Englisch bzw. (*AmE*) für amerikanisches Englisch gekennzeichnet.

Elisabeth Ström

Inhalt

An die LehrerIn	5
At the Tourist Office	9
At the Bank	30
At the Post Office	44
Shopping	59
Eating Out	72
Being Ill	87
At the Railway Station	101
Making Telephone Calls	120
Lösungen	145

An die LehrerIn

Die acht Kapitel des Bandes sind gleich aufgebaut und bestehen aus:

1. Wortliste
2. Phrasen
3. Dialoge
4. Overhead-Dialog mit deutschem und englischem Text
5. Pfeildialog
6. Rollenspiel
7. Test

Die einzelnen Übungsformen können der Reihe nach bearbeitet werden oder in der Auswahl bzw. Reihenfolge, die der Schülergruppe am besten entspricht. Zu den einzelnen Übungsformen:

1. Wortliste

Die Wortliste umfasst eine große Anzahl von Wörtern zum jeweiligen Themenbereich und ist daher keine Vokabelliste im herkömmlichen Sinn. Entsprechend dem Wissensstand der SchülerInnen können Sie aus folgenden Vorgangsweisen wählen:

- Geben Sie den SchülerInnen die ganze Liste und lassen Sie sie alle Wörter trainieren.
- Verwenden Sie die Wortliste als Hilfe zum selbstständigen Schreiben von Dialogen.
- Kopieren Sie die Wortliste auf eine Overhead-Folie und wählen Sie zusammen mit den SchülerInnen die Wörter aus, die wichtig erscheinen und daher gelernt werden sollen.
- Besprechen Sie mit der Gruppe (auf Deutsch), welche Wörter die SchülerInnen für den Themenbereich als notwendig erachten und geben Sie ihnen die englische Übersetzung dafür.

Das Bild eines menschlichen Körpers im Kapitel **Being Ill** ist als Hilfe zum Wörtertraining gedacht.

2. Phrasen

Hier finden Sie eine Reihe von englischen Redewendungen. Übersetzen Sie diese gemeinsam mit den SchülerInnen ins Deutsche. Zusammen mit anderen Redewendungen und Phrasen aus den Dialogen sollen die SchülerInnen damit eine Grundlage und Hilfe für das selbstständige Übersetzen von Dialogen und für die Rollenspiele erhalten.

3. Dialoge

In jedem Kapitel finden Sie zwei fertige Dialoge (mit Ausnahme des Kapitels **Making Telephone Calls**, in dem einige Kurzdialoge angeboten werden). Sie können allen SchülerInnen eine Kopie des Dialoges geben oder den Dialog auf Overhead-Folie darbieten. Lassen Sie die SchülerInnen den Dialog jeweils zu zweit trainieren. Dabei sollen die Rollen getauscht werden. Die Dialoge können auch als Grundlage zum Erstellen einer eigenen Liste von Wörtern und Redewendungen verwendet werden.

4. Overhead-Dialog mit deutschem und englischem Text

Diese Dialoge sind für den Overheadprojektor gedacht. Zum deutschen Dialog gibt es eine Direktübersetzung ins Englische.

Decken Sie den englischen Textteil ab und lassen Sie die SchülerInnen den deutschen Text lesen. Die SchülerInnen sollen Übersetzungsvorschläge bringen. Gehen Sie anschließend den Dialog Schritt für Schritt in beiden Sprachen durch. Lassen Sie die SchülerInnen den Dialog paarweise sprechen. Rollen tauschen!
Nach einigen Übungsdurchgängen decken Sie den englischen Textteil wieder ab. Die SchülerInnen sollen den englischen Dialog nur mithilfe des deutschen Textes sprechen.

5. Pfeildialog

Auch der Pfeildialog ist als Overhead-Übung gedacht. Dabei wird keine wortgetreue Übersetzung gefordert, sondern die SchülerInnen sollen den Inhalt des Dialogs selbst formulieren. Die vorher erlernten Redewendungen und Formulierungen (Dialog, Overhead-Dialog) können dabei angewendet werden.

Trainiert wird wieder mündlich zu zweit mit Rollentausch. Lassen Sie Dialog-Partner ihre Lösung der Aufgabe vortragen (evtl. vorher aufschreiben lassen) und sprechen Sie mit den SchülerInnen über die verschiedenen Lösungsmöglichkeiten.

6. Rollenspiel

- **Allgemein**

    Die Aufgabe des Rollenspiels ist es, im Klassenzimmer eine möglichst wirklichkeitsnahe Situation zu schaffen. Mithilfe von Schildern, eventuell Requisiten und etwas Fantasie verwandelt sich das Klassenzimmer in ein Postamt, eine Bank, ein Geschäft, einen Bahnhof usw.
    Bei einigen Rollenspielen erhalten die SchülerInnen Rollenspielkarten, die angeben, was zu sagen und zu tun ist. Das Rollenspiel gibt den SchülerInnen die Gelegenheit, das zuvor Geübte anzuwenden. Das Ziel ist, sich in Situationen, in die man bei einem Auslandsaufenthalt kommt, verständigen zu können.
    Mit einfachen Mitteln können die SchülerInnen „Wirklichkeit" spielen. Sie bekommen dadurch Gelegenheit, ihre sprachliche Sicherheit zu erhöhen und ihr Selbstvertrauen zu stärken. Darüber hinaus bietet das Rollenspiel eine lustige Abwechslung im Unterricht.

- **Tipps**

    Kopieren Sie die Schilder auf farbiges Papier. Anschließend können die Schilder foliert/laminiert oder in eine Klarsichthülle gesteckt werden. Das Folieren empfiehlt sich auch für die Rollenspielkarten, die man am besten auf etwas festeres Papier kopiert, damit sie länger halten.

- **At the Tourist Office**

    Inhalt:
    4 Schilder
    1 Stadtplan
    1 Hotelliste
    2 Listen mit Ausflugszielen
    Rollenspielkarten

    Verwandeln Sie das Klassenzimmer in ein Tourismusbüro, indem Sie das Schild *Tourist Information Centre* irgendwo gut sichtbar aufhängen. Drei SchülerInnen arbeiten in diesem Tourismusbüro. SchülerIn 1 begibt sich mit einem Stadtplan zum Schild *Information*, SchülerIn 2 mit einer Hotelliste und einem Stadtplan zum Schild *Accommodation* und SchülerIn 3 mit einem Stadtplan und den Listen der Ausflugsziele zum Schild *Guided Tours – Tickets*. Geben Sie allen übrigen SchülerInnen eine Rollenspielkarte. Sie sollen die geforderte Information an der richtigen Stelle einholen.

- **At the Bank**

    Inhalt:
    3 Schilder
    Reiseschecks in £
    Reiseschecks in $

    Vor Spielbeginn müssen die SchülerInnen über die Funktionsweise von Reiseschecks und den ungefähren Kurs von £ und $ informiert werden. Außerdem sollten sie wissen, welche verschiedenen Münzen und Geldscheine es in den beiden Währungen gibt (evtl. Tageskurse bei einer Bank erfragen). „Geldscheine" können aus farbigem Papier ausgeschnitten werden, oder man verwendet Spielgeld (aus der Spielwarenhandlung). Besonders geeignet sind natürlich übrig gebliebene Geldscheine und Münzen von einer England- bzw. Amerikareise.
    Hängen Sie die drei Schilder *Midland Bank, Thomas Cook* und *Exchange – Change – Cambio – Wechsel* an verschiedene Stellen des Klassenzimmers. Bei jedem Schild steht eine SchülerIn als Bankangestellte. Geben Sie den übrigen SchülerInnen (BankkundInnen) einige Geldscheine, Münzen und Reiseschecks. Das restliche Geld bekommen die Banken. Nun gehen die KundInnen in eine Bank und tätigen ihre Bankgeschäfte.

- **At the Post Office**

    Inhalt:
    6 Schilder

    Hängen Sie das Schild *Post Office* im Klassenzimmer auf. Ein bis vier SchülerInnen (je nach Gruppengröße) fungieren als PostbeamtInnen.

Nummerieren Sie dazu die „Schalter" mit den Ziffern 1, 2, 3 und 4. Bei einem der Schalter soll zusätzlich das Schild *Parcel Counter* angebracht werden. Kleine Poststellen in ländlichen Gegenden Großbritanniens werden oft in Zusammenhang mit einem Tabakladen o. Ä. geführt. In der Poststelle dieses Rollenspiels gibt es auch einen *Minishop*, in dem Papierwaren verkauft werden. Stellen Sie Ansichtskarten, Kuverts, Notizbücher, Papier und verschiedene Stifte zur Verfügung, sodass die SchülerInnen einkaufen können. Hängen Sie eine Preisliste zum Schild und geben Sie zu jeder Kasse ein Exemplar.

Die übrigen SchülerInnen stellen sich beim Schild *Queue here, please* in einer Schlange an und gehen dann eine nach der anderen zu einem freien Schalter. Sie können nach dem Porto fragen, Briefmarken kaufen, ein Paket abschicken oder Papierwaren kaufen.

- **Shopping**

    Inhalt:
    2 Schilder
    Rollenspielkarten

Ausgangspunkt ist ein Geschäft, eine KundIn, eine VerkäuferIn und eine Problemsituation (irgendetwas Unvorhergesehenes tritt ein, ähnlich wie in **Eating Out**). Beispiele für solche Problemsituationen finden Sie auf den verschiedenen Rollenspielkarten.

Die SchülerInnen sollen paarweise einen Dialog erarbeiten und aufschreiben, den sie anschließend der Klasse vorspielen. Dabei kann eine Situation frei erfunden werden oder auf die Rollenspielkarten zurückgegriffen werden. Vor dem Vorführen der Dialoge werden die Schilder *Sale* und *Fitting Room* aufgehängt. Zusätzliche Requisiten, z. B. verschiedene Waren, beleben die Spielsituation. Es kann aber auch rein pantomimisch gespielt werden.

- **Eating Out**

    Inhalt:
    2 Speisekarten
    Rollenspielkarten

Schreiben Sie den Namen eines Restaurants an die Tafel. Wenn Sie die Speisekarte *The Bull and Dragon* verwenden, schreiben Sie natürlich diesen Namen an die Tafel. Fügen Sie einige Fakten, z. B. *Opening Hours…* und *Today's Special…* an. „Möblieren" Sie den Platz vor der Tafel als Restaurant. Um eine entsprechende Stimmung zu schaffen, können Sie farbige A4-Blätter als Tischsets verwenden, eine Lampe, Blumen oder Ähnliches aufstellen. Geben Sie den SchülerInnen eine der Speisekarten. Zu Beginn können Sie selbst als KellnerIn fungieren und die SchülerInnen bestellen und bezahlen lassen.

Als nächsten Schritt sollen die SchülerInnen paarweise eigene Dialoge schreiben, die sie dann der Klasse vorspielen. Ausgangspunkt ist ein Restaurant, eine KellnerIn, ein Gast und eine Problemsituation (irgendetwas Unvorhergesehenes tritt ein, wie in **Shopping**). Beispiele für solche Problemsituationen finden Sie auf den verschiedenen Rollenspielkarten. Ein Teil der SchülerInnen zieht es vielleicht vor, sich selbst entsprechende Situationen auszudenken und eigene Dialoge zu gestalten, während andere die Rollenspielkarten als Hilfe verwenden.

- **Being Ill**

    Inhalt:
    Rollenspielkarten mit Namen von Krankheiten
    Rollenspielkarten mit Namen von Arzneien

Gestalten Sie die Klasse als Apotheke. Schreiben Sie z. B. *Boots. Dispensing Chemist* an die Tafel. Als Ladentisch kann eine Bank oder ein Tisch verwendet werden. Die Kärtchen mit den Namen der Arzneien können entweder auf leeren Pillendosen, Arzneiflaschen o. Ä. befestigt oder einfach aufgelegt werden. Eine SchülerIn arbeitet als ApothekerIn und hat ein Sortiment von Arzneien (oder nur Arznei-Kärtchen) vor sich auf dem Ladentisch.

Die Karten mit den Namen der Krankheiten behalten Sie in der Hand. Sagen Sie z. B.: „Have an illness!", und lassen Sie eine SchülerIn nach der anderen eine Karte ziehen. Jede SchülerIn geht dann in die Apotheke, erklärt, was ihr fehlt, und kauft die entsprechende Arznei.

- **At the Railway Station**

    Inhalt:
    3 Schilder
    2 Fahrpläne
    1 Zeichenerklärung
    Rollenspielkarten – einfache Variante
    Rollenspielkarten – schwierige Variante

Das Klassenzimmer kann sich leicht in eine Bahnhofshalle verwandeln, indem Sie die Schilder *Penalty Fares* und *Safety Message* aufhängen. Außerdem können Sie einige Schilder an die Tafel zeichnen, z. B. *Toilets* → und ← *To the Trains*. Je nach Gruppengröße arbeiten entweder eine oder mehrere SchülerInnen als Bahnbedienstete beim Schild *Tickets & Information*. Jede von ihnen bekommt eine Kopie des Fahrplanes und der Zeichenerklärungen.

Die übrigen SchülerInnen erhalten Rollenspielkarten mit Aufträgen. Die Rollenspielkarten sind in zwei Varianten verfügbar: eine Variante mit leichten, einfachen Fragen und eine zweite, bei der mehr Information einzuholen ist.

- **Making Telephone Calls**

    Inhalt:
    3 *Piece It Together*-Dialoge mit dazugehörigen Rollenspielkarten
    Rollenspielkarten – deutsche Version
    Rollenspielkarten – englische Version

Es ist oft schwieriger, ein Telefongespräch zu führen, als sich mit einem im Raum anwesenden Gesprächspartner zu unterhalten. Deshalb wurde dieses Kapitel um einige zusätzliche Übungen erweitert.

Bei den *Piece It Together*-Dialogen bekommen die SchülerInnen Rollenspielkarten mit Äußerungen von Telefongesprächspartnern, die zu einem Dialog zusammengesetzt werden sollen. Jeweils zwei SchülerInnen erhalten die Rollenspielkarten eines Dialoges in ungeordneter Reihenfolge. Sie müssen den Inhalt des Telefonates herausfinden und die Karten anschließend richtig ordnen. Zur Überprüfung steht ein Kontrollblatt mit dem vollständigen, geordneten Dialog zur Verfügung. Der zusammengestellte Dialog soll paarweise mündlich trainiert werden, wobei die Rollen getauscht werden.

Dieses Kapitel beinhaltet eine weitere Rollenspielvariante: Die SchülerInnen arbeiten wieder paarweise. Eine SchülerIn ist Nr. 1 und bekommt z. B. die Rollenspielkarte A 1. Die zweite SchülerIn ist Nr. 2 und bekommt in diesem Fall die Karte A 2. Die SchülerIn mit der Nummer 1 ist immer diejenige, die anruft. Auf den Karten ist jeweils angegeben, aus welchem Grund Nr. 1 anruft und was Nr. 2 antwortet. Die SchülerInnen sollen daraus ein möglichst wirklichkeitsnahes Telefongespräch improvisieren.

Die Rollenspielkarten gibt es sowohl in englischer als auch deutscher Sprache, für jede Sprache gibt es auch ein Zusammenfassungsblatt für die LehrerIn. Sie können für Ihre Gruppe das Geeignete wählen. Bei der englischen Version sind Wörter und Ausdrücke für das Gespräch vorgegeben, während bei der deutschen Variante von den SchülerInnen selbstständig übersetzt werden muss.

7. Test

Den Abschluss jedes Kapitels bildet ein Test, bei dem die SchülerInnen nach deutschen Vorgaben einen englischen Dialog zum jeweiligen Thema gestalten, ähnlich wie bei den Pfeildialogen. Die Lösungen für die Tests finden Sie am Ende des Buches. Bitte beachten Sie beim Korrigieren, dass es oft mehrere richtige Lösungsmöglichkeiten gibt. Rechtschreib- oder Grammatikfehlern sollte keine große Bedeutung beigemessen werden. Wichtig ist, dass sich die SchülerInnen in englischer Sprache ausdrücken und Informationen einholen und geben können. Selbstverständlich kann der Test auch als zusätzliche Übung angeboten und von den SchülerInnen selbst korrigiert werden.

Da es der Hauptzweck dieses Materials ist, den mündlichen Sprachgebrauch zu aktivieren und zu fördern, kann ein abschließender Test auch in Form eines Rollenspiels erfolgen. Die LehrerIn führt z. B. als BankbeamtIn, VerkäuferIn usw. ein Gespräch mit der SchülerIn als KundIn und überprüft so deren Kenntnisse.

At the Tourist Office

staatliche britische Tourismusbehörde	—	BTA (British Tourist Authority /ɔːˈθɒrəti/)
Tourismusbüro, Touristeninformation	—	tourist information office/centre, tourist office, visitor centre, travel centre
TouristIn	—	tourist
Tourismus	—	tourism
Reisebüro	—	travel agency/bureau /ˈbjʊərəʊ/, travel agent's
Angestellte in einem Reisebüro	—	travel agent
BesucherIn	—	visitor
besuchen	—	visit
Reisende	—	traveller
reisen (*verb*)	—	travel
Reise (*substantiv*)	—	journey /ˈdʒɜːni/, travel
kurze Reise	—	trip
Ausflug	—	excursion /ɪkˈskɜːʃn/, outing
Rundreise, Rundtour	—	tour
Besichtigungsrundfahrt	—	sightseeing tour
Kreuzfahrt	—	cruise
Flug	—	flight
Autofahrt	—	ride, drive
reisekrank	—	travel-sick
Reisekrankheit	—	travel sickness
Karte	—	map
Broschüre	—	leaflet, brochure /ˈbrəʊʃə/
Reiseführer (Buch)	—	guide book
Souvenir	—	souvenir /ˌsuːvəˈnɪə/
Gutschein	—	voucher /ˈvaʊtʃə/
Unterkunft	—	accommodation /əˈkɒməˈdeɪʃn/
Hotel	—	hotel

At the Tourist Office

Zimmer mit Frühstück	—	bed and breakfast, B&B
Pension	—	guest house
Gasthof	—	inn
Jugendherberge	—	youth hostel /ˈjuːθˌhɒstl/
Campingplatz	—	camp/camping site, camping ground
Karte, Ticket	—	ticket
Eintrittskarte	—	entrance ticket

At the Tourist Office

Asking the Way

hinter	—	behind
vor	—	in front /frʌnt/ of
gegenüber	—	opposite
bei	—	by, at
neben	—	beside, next to
außerhalb, draußen	—	outside
innerhalb, drinnen	—	inside
(quer) über	—	across
nach rechts	—	to the right
nach links	—	to the left
auf der rechten Seite	—	on/to your right
auf der linken Seite	—	on/to your left
nach rechts abbiegen	—	turn right
nach links abbiegen	—	turn left
geradeaus	—	straight on/ahead
Straße	—	street
(Land)Straße	—	road
Gasse	—	lane
Sackgasse	—	cul-de-sac /ˈkʌl də ˌsæk/, blind alley /ˌblaɪnd ˈæli/
Abzweigung	—	turning, crossroad
Hauptstraße, Allee	—	avenue
Autobahn	—	motorway
Kreisverkehr	—	roundabout
Ampel	—	traffic lights
Zebrastreifen	—	zebra /ˈzebrə/ crossing
Kreuzung	—	crossroads, junction /ˈdʒʌŋkʃən/

At the Tourist Office

- Do you know if there's a tourist information centre nearby?

- Excuse me, please, how do I get to …?
- I've lost my way.
- It's just around the corner.
- You can't miss it.
- Could you show me on the map, please?

- Can you help us find accommodation for the night?

- Do you sell guide books and maps?

- Are there any sightseeing tours?

- Have you got a guide to theatre, sightseeing and events?

- Are there any places of particular interest nearby?

- I'd like a timetable for the local buses, please.

At the Tourist Office

Dialogue 1

(In the street)

A   Excuse me, how do I get to the tourist information centre, please?

B   Go along this street until you come to the roundabout. Turn left into Park Lane. Walk past the first set of traffic lights. Turn right and go over the bridge. Walk straight on for another 50 yards and it's there on your right. You can't miss it!

A   Could you show me on the map, please?

B   Certainly!

- - - - - - - - - - -

A   Thank you.

B   Can you remember it all?

A   Hopefully, yes.

B   Well, goodbye then.

A   Bye.

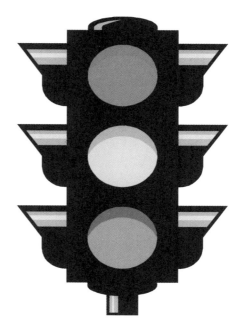

At the Tourist Office

Dialogue 2

(At the Tourist Office)

A   Can I help you?

B   I wonder if there are any guided tours.

A   What do you have in mind, a sightseeing tour or a day tour?

B   A day tour.

A   Well, you can go to the Isle of Wight, Arundel Castle and Chichester, Lewes, Bodiam and Leeds Castle or Dieppe in France.

B   How much is the tour to Arundel Castle and Chichester?

A   Let me see … £25.00 including lunch.

B   That sounds good. I'd like two tickets for tomorrow, please. Where does the coach leave from, and what time?

A   It leaves at 9.30 in the morning outside this office.

B   Do you have any information about these places?

A   Yes, certainly. There are some leaflets and maps down in the corner. They're free. Here are your tickets.

B   Thank you. Goodbye.

A   Have a nice day out! Bye!

At the Tourist Office

(Auf der Straße)

A Entschuldigen Sie bitte, können Sie mir sagen, wo das Hotel Atlantic ist?

B Gehen Sie geradeaus bis zur zweiten Ampel. Dann biegen Sie rechts ab. Das Hotel ist gegenüber der Bank of England.

A Ist es weit?

B Nein, gar nicht, ungefähr 15 Minuten zu Fuß.

A Gibt es einen Bus dorthin?

B Leider nicht, aber auf der anderen Seite ist ein Taxistand.

A Danke schön! Auf Wiedersehen!

B Auf Wiedersehen!

A *Excuse me, could you please tell me where the Atlantic (hotel) is?*

B *Go straight on until the second set of traffic lights. Turn right. The hotel is opposite the Bank of England.*

A *Is it far?*

B *No, not at all. It's about 15 minutes' walk.*

A *Are there any buses?*

B *I'm afraid not, but there's a taxi rank on the other side of the street.*

A *Thank you very much. Goodbye.*

B *Goodbye.*

At the Tourist Office

A Grüßen Sie und sagen Sie, dass Sie gerne einige Information über London hätten.

B Sagen Sie, dass es Gratisbroschüren unten an der Ecke gibt, dass Sie aber einen ausgezeichneten Reiseführer um nur £3.50 anbieten können.

A Bitten Sie, diesen Reiseführer sehen zu können.

B Sagen Sie, dass Sie ihn holen werden. Geben Sie A den Reiseführer.

A Sagen Sie, dass Sie ihn gut finden. Fragen Sie B, ob es auch einen Theater- und Veranstaltungsführer gibt.

B Sagen Sie, dass Sie einen zum Preis von 85 pence anbieten können.

A Sagen Sie, dass Sie beides nehmen.

B Sagen Sie, wie viel es zusammen kostet.

A Fragen Sie, ob es in den Nähe eine Jugendherberge gibt.

B Sagen Sie, dass sich die Jugendherberge hinter dem Bahnhof befindet.

A Bedanken und verabschieden Sie sich.

B Verabschieden Sie sich.

At the Tourist Office

Tourist Information Centre

At the Tourist Office

Information

At the Tourist Office

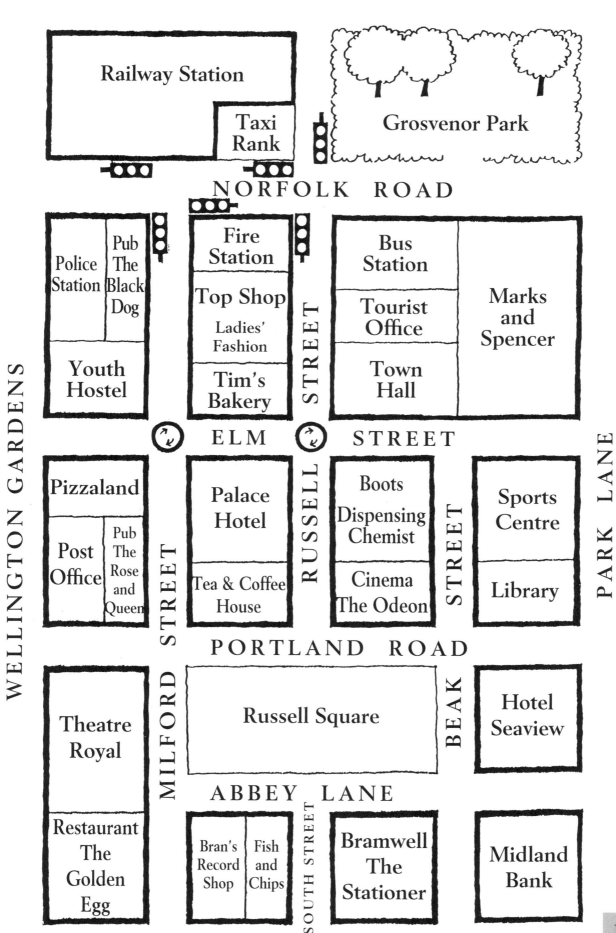

At the Tourist Office

Accommodation

At the Tourist Office

Hotels and Guest Houses

Palace Hotel

32–36 Milford Street   *Tel:* 567 093

B&B per person x 1 night   £25.00
B&B per person x 7 nights £160.00

All rooms have: private bathroom, TV and radio

Carlton Court Hotel

15 Church Lane   *Tel:* 731 168

B&B per person x 1 night   £20.00
B&B per person x 7 nights £140.00

good parking facilities, best seafront position

Regent House

141 Brompton Street   *Tel:* 703 018

B&B per person x 1 night   £18.00
B&B per person x 7 nights £115.00

indoor swimming pool, private garage

Hotel Seaview

8 Beak Street   *Tel:* 811 203

B&B per person x 1 night   £15.00
B&B per person x 7 nights £95.00

no dogs allowed

At the Tourist Office

Guided Tours

Tickets

At the Tourist Office

Guided Tours – Sightseeing

"London Extra" (guided bus tour)

Approx. 2 hours

Price: £10.95 (including entrance fees)

A Cruise along the River Thames

Approx. 55 min

Price: £6.50

Historical Pub Walk

Approx. 3 hours

Price: £5.75

London by Night

Approx. 2 hours

Price: £9.25

The Grand Tour of London

Full day

Price: £25.75 (incl. entrance fees and lunch)

At the Tourist Office

Guided Tours – Day Tours

All entrance fees are included in the price.

Oxford & Stratford-on-Avon
Full day

Price: £28.00 (including lunch)

Stonehenge
Full day

Price: £18.00 (including lunch)

Brighton & Hove
Full day

Price: £21.75 (lunch not included)

Windsor Castle
Full day

Price: £20.00 (lunch not included)

At the Tourist Office

Role Cards

You want a single room for two nights.	You would like a map of the town.
You would like to go on a sightseeing tour.	You want to cash some traveller's cheques.
You would like to go on a day tour, but don't know where to go.	You want to know where the Sports Centre is.
You want to know where the Youth Hostel is.	You would like to go out for a meal.

At the Tourist Office

Role Cards

You're looking for somewhere to stay the night.	You want to know where the nearest chemist's is.
You need to buy stamps for some postcards.	You would like to play squash.
You want to know where the police station is, because your car has been broken into.	You would like to know what there is to do in the evenings.
You need to buy some envelopes.	You are looking for South Street.

At the Tourist Office

Role Cards

You're looking for Hotel Seaview.	You would like to play tennis.
You would like a timetable for the local buses.	You would like to go to Brighton for the day.
You want to know if there's a riding school nearby.	You want to know if there are any places of interest nearby.
You would like to go on a tour to Stratford-on-Avon.	You want to know the way to Bran's Record Shop.

At the Tourist Office

Test Paper

Express yourself in good English.

(Auf der Straße)

A   Fragen Sie B, wo das Tourismusbüro ist.

B   Erklären Sie A, sie soll geradeaus bis zur Ampel gehen, dort nach rechts abbiegen, weitergehen, bis sie zu einem Park kommt, und diesen Park durchqueren. Sagen Sie, dass sich das Tourismusbüro neben der Kirche befindet.

A   Bitten Sie B, den Weg auf dem Plan zu zeigen.

B   Antworten Sie: „Ja, gerne!" Sagen Sie, dass der Weg nicht weit ist.

A   Bedanken Sie sich.

At the Tourist Office

(Im Tourismusbüro)

A   Fragen Sie, ob es in der Nähe interessante Ausflugsziele gibt.

C   Sagen Sie A, dass sie nach Land's End, St. Ives oder Penzance fahren kann.

A   Fragen Sie, was eine geführte Tour nach St. Ives kostet.

C   Nennen Sie einen Preis und sagen Sie, dass dieser Preis das Mittagessen einschließt.

A   Fragen Sie, ob Sie morgen fahren können.

C   Sagen Sie, dass das möglich ist und dass der Bus um 9.00 Uhr abfährt.

A   Kaufen Sie drei Tickets.

C   Nennen Sie den Preis für die Tickets und überreichen Sie A die Tickets zusammen mit einer Gratisbroschüre über St. Ives.

A   Bedanken und verabschieden Sie sich.

C   Verabschieden Sie sich.

At the Bank

Bank	—	bank
Wechselstube	—	bureau de change /ˌbjʊərəʊ də ˈʃɒndʒ/, exchange /ɪksˈtʃeɪndʒ/ office
(Geld)Schein	—	(bank)note (*BrE*), bill (*AmE*)
Münze	—	coin
Brieftasche	—	wallet
Geldbörse	—	purse
Reisescheck	—	traveller's cheque
Kreditkarte	—	credit card
Bargeld	—	cash
Bankkonto	—	bank account
Scheckkonto	—	cheque account
Scheck	—	cheque
Sparbuch	—	bank book
ein Konto eröffnen	—	open an account
auf ein Konto einzahlen	—	pay into a bank account
Geld abheben	—	withdraw money
Geldbehebung	—	withdrawal /wɪðˈdrɔːəl/
Kontoauszug	—	bank statement
Zinsen	—	interest
Bankgebühren	—	bank charge
Banküberweisung	—	bank transfer
Quittung	—	receipt /rɪˈsiːt/
Formular	—	form
Reisepass	—	passport
Personalausweis	—	identity card
Barzahlung	—	cash payment
Wechselgeld	—	change money
Verkaufskurs	—	selling rate
Einkaufskurs	—	buying rate

At the Bank

Kommission, Provision	—	commission
KassierIn	—	cashier /kæˈʃɪə/
unterschreiben	—	sign
gegenzeichnen	—	countersign
Tresor	—	safe
Tresor(raum)	—	strong-room
Bankschließfach	—	safe-deposit box

At the Bank

- Excuse me, can you tell me where the nearest bank/bureau de change is?

- I'd like to change these dollars into pounds.

- I'd like to cash some traveller's cheques.

- What's the exchange rate, please?
- Is there any commission?
- How much commission do you charge?

- Do you have any proof of identity?

- Can I see your passport, please?

- Will you sign here, please?
- How would you like the money?
- I'd like two fives and four tens, please.

- I'd like to withdraw some money from my account.

At the Bank

Dialogue 1

A Good morning. Can I help you?

B Yes, I'd like to cash these traveller's cheques, please.

A Certainly. How much for?

B 100 dollars.

A Do you have any proof of identity?

[...] the date here and countersign [...]

[...] like the money?

[...]ns, please.

At the Bank

Dialogue 2

(In the street)

A   Excuse me, sir. Do you know if there's a bank nearby?

B   No, but there's a bureau de change just down the road.

A   Thank you.

B   Not at all. Goodbye!

(At the bureau de change)

A   Good morning. Can I cash traveller's cheques here?

C   Yes, certainly. Just countersign here, … and your passport, please.

A   Here you are.

C   Thank you. Here's your money, … fifty pounds.

A   Thanks. By the way, is it possible to open an account here?

C   No, I'm afraid not. You'll have to go to the bank. Midland Bank is in Eton Street, and you'll find Barclay's Bank in Russell Street. It's not very far.

A   Thank you very much. Goodbye!

C   Thank you. Bye!

Samstag 6. Januar
Open House

ab 20 Uhr

Music, Fun, Talk, Snack

Special:

Gäste aus Costa Rica, England, Irland, Kanada, Ukraine und USA;

RC./ Dr. Külz-Str. 21: gegenüber Wohnheim Ingenieurschule

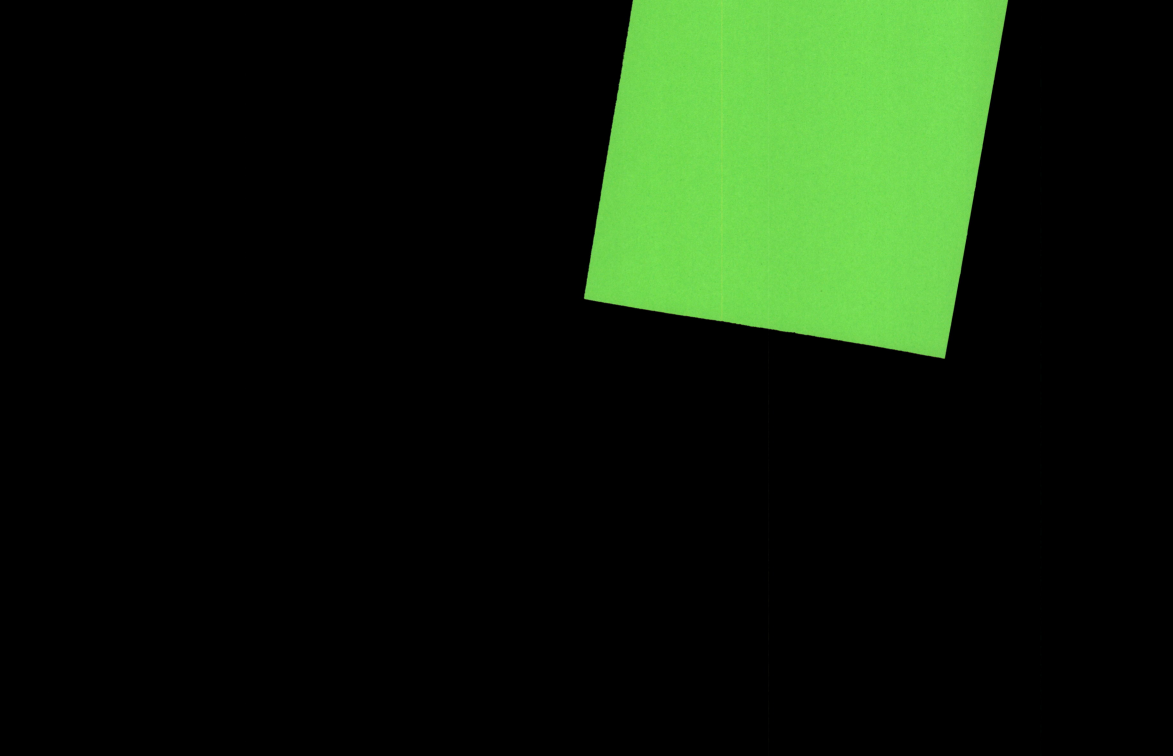

At the Bank

A Guten Tag!

B Guten Tag!

A Ich möchte einige Reiseschecks einlösen.

B Bitte gerne!

A Muss ich Provision bezahlen?

B Ja, 2 %.

A Ich möchte diese beiden Schecks einlösen.

B Natürlich! Kann ich Ihren Reisepass sehen?

A Bitte sehr.

B Danke! Wie möchten Sie das Geld haben?

A Fünf Zehner und zehn Fünfer, bitte.

B Bitte sehr, hier sind 100 £.

A Danke und auf Wiedersehen.

B Auf Wiedersehen! Einen schönen Nachmittag noch!

A *Good afternoon!*

B *Good afternoon!*

A *I'd like to cash some traveller's cheques, please.*

B *Yes, certainly.*

A *Is there any commission?*

B *Yes, 2 %.*

A *I'd like to cash these two cheques then, please.*

B *Of course! Can I have your passport, please?*

A *Here you are.*

B *Thank you. How would you like the money?*

A *Five tens and ten fives, please.*

B *Here you are, £100.*

A *Thank you very much. Goodbye.*

B *Bye. Have a nice afternoon!*

At the Bank

A Grüßen Sie und fragen Sie, womit Sie helfen können.

B Sagen Sie, dass Sie einige Reiseschecks einlösen möchten.

A Antworten Sie, dass das möglich ist. Fragen Sie, wie hoch die Geldsumme ist.

B Antworten Sie darauf.

A Wiederholen Sie die Summe. Bitten Sie die KundIn, auf jeden Reisescheck den Namen, den Ort und das Datum zu schreiben.

B Antworten Sie darauf.

A Sagen Sie der KundIn, dass sie für die Schecks 100 Pfund bekommt. Fragen Sie, wie sie das Geld haben möchte.

B Sagen Sie, dass Sie das nicht verstehen.

A Erlären Sie, was Sie meinen.

B Sagen Sie, welche Geldscheine Sie haben möchten.

A Zählen Sie der KundIn das Geld vor und geben Sie es ihr.

B Bedanken und verabschieden Sie sich.

A Verabschieden Sie sich.

At the Bank

Traveller's Cheques

Signature　　　　　　　　　　Place　　　　　　　Date

£20.00　　　*Thomas Cook*
Twenty pounds

Countersign here

Signature　　　　　　　　　　Place　　　　　　　Date

£50.00　　　*Thomas Cook*
Fifty pounds

Countersign here

Signature　　　　　　　　　　Place　　　　　　　Date

£100.00　　　*Thomas Cook*
One hundred pounds

Countersign here

At the Bank

Traveller's Cheques

Signature   Place   Date

$20.00   **American Express**
Twenty dollars

Countersign here

Signature   Place   Date

$50.00   **American Express**
Fifty dollars

Countersign here

Signature   Place   Date

$100.00   **American Express**
One hundred dollars

Countersign here

At the Bank

Thomas Cook

At the Bank

Midland Bank

At the Bank

Exchange
Change
Cambio
Wechsel

At the Bank

Test Paper

Express yourself in good English.

A Grüßen Sie und fragen Sie, ob Sie einige Reiseschecks einlösen können.

B Sagen Sie, dass das möglich ist und fragen Sie, um welche Summe es sich handelt.

A Nennen Sie den Betrag.

B Fragen Sie A nach einem Ausweis.

A Sagen Sie, dass Sie Ihren Reisepass dabei haben.

B Bitten Sie, ihn sehen zu dürfen.

A Sagen Sie: „Gerne!"

B Erklären Sie A, wo auf dem Scheck der Ort und das Datum zu schreiben sind und wo gegengezeichnet werden muss.

At the Bank

A Überreichen Sie den Reisescheck.

B Fragen Sie A, wie sie das Geld haben will.

A Sagen Sie, wie Sie das Geld haben wollen.

B Geben Sie A das Geld und den Reisepass.

A Bedanken und verabschieden Sie sich.

B Verabschieden Sie sich.

At the Post Office

Postamt	—	post office
Brief	—	letter
Postkarte	—	postcard
Briefmarke	—	stamp
Briefumschlag	—	envelope /ˈenvələup/
Paket	—	parcel
Briefpapier	—	notepaper
Adresse	—	address /əˈdres/
Porto	—	postage /ˈpəustɪdʒ/
Absender	—	sender
Briefkasten	—	letter box (*BrE*), (mail)box (*AmE*)
Briefträger	—	postman
Postleitzahl	—	postcode
Poststempel	—	postmark
Postfach	—	post office box, PO Box
Zustellung	—	delivery /dɪˈlɪvəri/ (of mail)
Schalter	—	post office counter
Priority (Auslandspost)	—	1st class
Non-Priority (Auslandspost)	—	2nd class
Brieffreund	—	pen friend
Nachnahme	—	cash on delivery
eingeschriebener Brief	—	registered /ˈredʒɪstəd/ letter
Postanweisung	—	money order
Aufgabeschein	—	dispatch note /dɪˈspætʃ nəut/
Postanweisungsformular	—	money order form
(Geld)Schein	—	(bank)note (*BrE*), bill (*AmE*)
Münze	—	coin

At the Post Office

Brieftasche	—	wallet
Geldbörse	—	purse
Personalausweis	—	identity card
Reisepass	—	passport
Luftpost	—	airmail
Postgiroformular	—	(postal) giro /dʒaɪrəʊ/ form
Postgirokonto	—	postal giro account
Zollerklärung	—	customs declaration

At the Post Office

- Excuse me, could you please tell me where the nearest post office is?

- Is there a letter box nearby?

- Do you sell stamps and envelopes?

- I need five 30p stamps, please.

- 1st or 2nd class?
- What's the postage for these letters to Greece?

- I'd like to send this parcel to London.

- How long will it take for a 1st class letter to reach Germany?

- How much is it to send a letter by airmail to Austria?

- Can I have ten 1st class stamps for Austria, please?

Samstag 6. Januar
Open House

ab 20 Uhr

Music, Fun, Talk, Snack

Special:

Gäste aus Costa Rica, England, Irland,
Kanada, Ukraine und USA;

RC./ Dr. Külz-Str. 21: gegenüber Wohnheim Ingenieurschule

At the Post Office

Dialogue 1

(In the street)

A   Excuse me, sir. Could you tell me where the nearest post office is, please?

B   Of course. Turn left here, go straight on until you come to the traffic lights. Turn right and it's there on your right hand side.

A   Thank you very much, goodbye.

B   Goodbye.

(In the post office)

A   Good morning.

C   Good morning. Can I help you?

A   Yes, please. I'd like to buy some stamps.

C   Where to?

A   Well, I've got two letters for Austria and one for the United States.

C   1st or 2nd class?

A   1st class, please. It's quicker, isn't it?

C   Yes, it is. That'll be £1.23.

A   Here you are, £2.

C   Thank you. Here's your change, and your stamps, don't forget them!

A   No, I won't! Thank you very much. Goodbye!

At the Post Office

Dialogue 2

A Good afternoon.

B Good afternoon. What can I do for you?

A I'd like to send this parcel to France.

B 1st or 2nd class?

A 1st class, please.

B Let me see, that'll be £2.80.

A £2.80, here you are. And do you sell envelopes?

B I'm afraid we don't. You'll have to go to the stationer's, it's just across the road.

A Oh, I see. Thank you very much then. Goodbye.

B Bye. Have a nice afternoon!

PUB

Samstag 6. Januar
Open House

ab 20 Uhr

Music, Fun, Talk, Snack

Special:

Gäste aus Costa Rica, England, Irland,
Kanada, Ukraine und USA;

RC./ Dr. Külz-Str. 21: gegenüber Wohnheim Ingenieurschule

At the Post Office

A	Guten Morgen!	A	*Good morning.*
B	Guten Morgen!	B	*Good morning.*
A	Ich möchte diese Postkarten aufgeben.	A	*I would like to send these postcards, please.*
B	Wohin?	B	*Where to?*
A	Drei nach Österreich und eine nach Frankreich.	A	*Three to Austria and two to France.*
B	Priority oder Non-Priority?	B	*1st or 2nd class?*
A	Priority, bitte.	A	*1st class, please.*
B	Das macht 30 p pro Karte.	B	*That'll be 30p each.*
A	Dann möchte ich zehn 30-Pence-Marken.	A	*Then I'd like ten 30p stamps, please.*
B	Bitte sehr. Das macht 3 Pfund.	B	*Here you are. That'll be £3.00.*
A	Vielen Dank! Auf Wiedersehen!	A	*Thank you very much. Goodbye!*
B	Auf Wiedersehen!	B	*Bye!*

At the Post Office

A Grüßen Sie.

          B Grüßen Sie.

A Sagen Sie, Sie wollen etwas abschicken.

          B Antworten Sie, dass das möglich ist. Fragen Sie, wohin.

A Antworten Sie auf die Frage.

          B Fragen Sie, ob es Priority oder Non-Priority sein soll.

A Antworten Sie darauf. Außerdem möchten Sie ein Kuvert kaufen.

          B Antworten Sie, dass Sie keine Kuverts verkaufen. Sagen Sie A, dass es Kuverts in der Papierhandlung um die Ecke gibt.

A Antworten Sie darauf. Fragen Sie, wie viel Porto Sie bezahlen müssen.

          B Antworten Sie darauf.

A Bezahlen Sie.

          B Danken Sie und geben Sie das Wechselgeld zurück.

A Bedanken und verabschieden Sie sich.

          B Verabschieden Sie sich.

At the Post Office

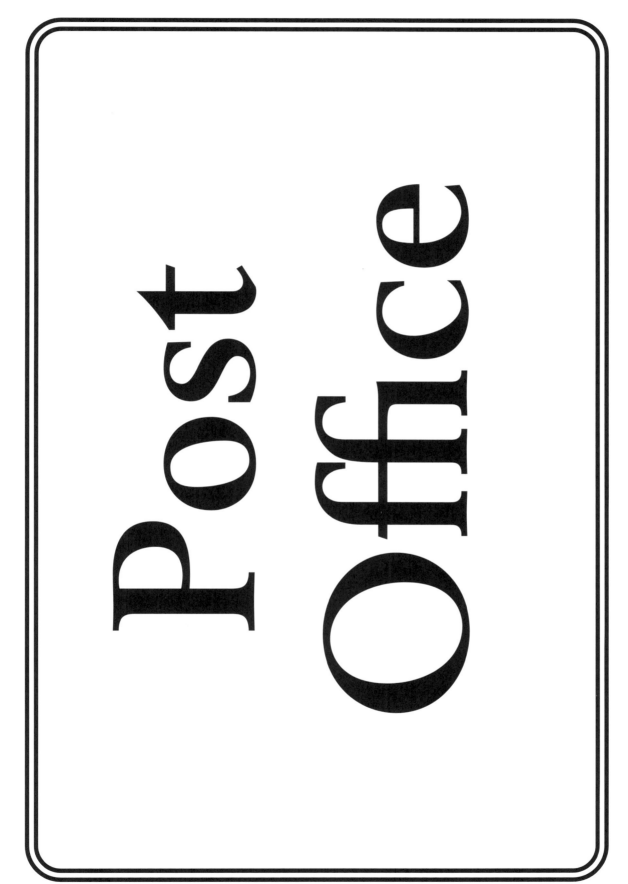

At the Post Office

Queue here, please

Kopiervorlage • Excuse me, please …
©VERITAS-Verlag ISBN 3-7058-5557-3

At the Post Office

1	2
3	4

At the Post Office

Parcel Counter

At the Post Office

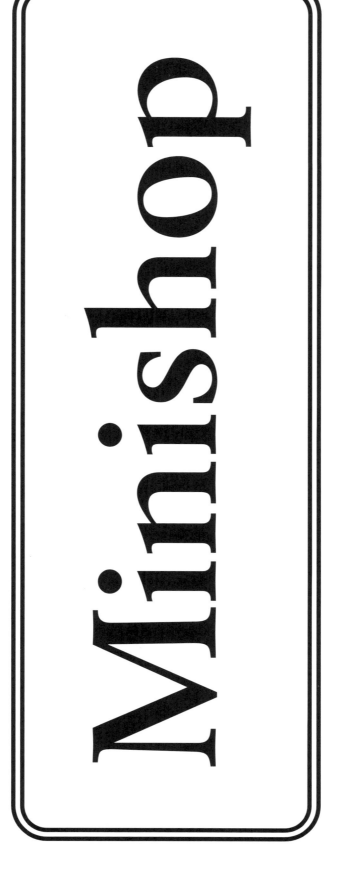

At the Post Office

Minishop

Price-list

Postcard		50p
Envelope,	small	20p
	large	30p
Notebook,	small	70p
	large	95p
Coloured paper (per sheet)		10p
Coloured pencil		45p
Pencil		35p
Pen		70p

At the Post Office

Test Paper

Express yourself in good English.

A   Grüßen Sie.

B   Grüßen Sie und fragen Sie, womit Sie helfen können.

A   Sagen Sie, dass Sie einige Briefe und Ansichtskarten aufgeben möchten.

B   Fragen Sie nach dem Bestimmungsland.

A   Sagen Sie, dass es zwei Briefe nach Österreich, einer nach Spanien und drei Ansichtskarten nach Deutschland sind.

B   Frage Sie, ob es Priority oder Non-Priority sein soll.

A   Fragen Sie, wie lange es dauert, bis die Post ankommt.

B   Sagen Sie, dass es drei Tage mit Priority und ca. 1 Woche mit Non-Priority dauert.

At the Post Office

A Sagen Sie, dass Sie sechs Briefmarken für Priority möchten.

B Geben Sie A die Marken und sagen Sie: „Bitte schön!" Sagen Sie, wie viel es kostet.

A Bezahlen Sie mit einem Geldschein, dessen Wert höher ist als der Betrag. (Sie haben kein Kleingeld.)

B Geben Sie das Wechselgeld zurück. Sagen Sie, wie groß der Retourbetrag ist.

A Bedanken Sie sich und fragen Sie, wo sich der nächste Postkasten befindet.

B Sagen Sie, dass er dort drüben an der Ecke ist.

A Bedanken und verabschieden Sie sich.

B Verabschieden Sie sich.

Shopping

Geschäft, Laden	—	shop *(BrE)*, store *(AmE)*
Warenhaus	—	department store
KundIn	—	customer /ˈkʌstəmə/
VerkäuferIn	—	shop assistant
Einkaufszentrum	—	shopping centre, shopping precinct /ˈpriːsiŋkt/, (shopping) mall *(AmE)*
Einkaufswagen	—	shopping trolley /ˈtrɒli/
einkaufen	—	shop, do one's shopping
kaufen	—	buy
bezahlen	—	pay
Bargeld	—	cash
bar bezahlen	—	pay in cash
(Geld)Schein	—	(bank)note *(BrE)*, bill *(AmE)*
Münze	—	coin
Kreditkarte	—	credit card
mit Scheck zahlen	—	pay by cheque
einen Scheck ausstellen	—	write out a cheque
Rabatt	—	discount /ˈdɪskaʊnt/
Sonderangebot	—	special offer
Aus-, Schlussverkauf	—	sale, bargain /ˈbɑːgɪn/ sale
Sonderpreis	—	bargain price
ein Schnäppchen machen	—	make a bargain
Ladentisch	—	counter
Kasse	—	cash desk, pay desk
Registrierkasse	—	cash register /ˈredʒɪstə/
KassierIn	—	cashier /kæˈʃɪə/
Rechnung	—	receipt /rɪˈsiːt/
stehlen, klauen	—	shoplift
Ladendiebstahl	—	shoplifting
Ladendieb	—	shoplifter
Handtasche	—	handbag, purse
Brieftasche	—	wallet
Geldbörse	—	purse
Umkleidekabine	—	fitting room
anprobieren	—	try on

Shopping

Shops

Süßwarengeschäft	—	sweet shop
Blumenhandlung	—	florist's (shop)
Buchhandlung	—	bookshop
Zeitungsgeschäft	—	newsagent's
Bäckerei	—	baker's
Fleischhauerei, Metzgerei	—	butcher's
Obst- u. Gemüsegeschäft	—	greengrocer's
Fischgeschäft	—	fishmonger's /ˈfɪʃmʌŋgəz/
Lebensmittelgeschäft	—	grocer's
Supermarkt, SB-Laden	—	supermarket, self-service shop
Papierhandlung	—	stationer's
Eisenwarenhandlung	—	ironmonger's /ˈaɪənmʌŋgəz/ (*BrE*), hardware store (*AmE*)
Schuhgeschäft	—	shoe shop
Juwelier	—	jeweller's /ˈdʒuːələz/
Optiker	—	optician's /ɒpˈtɪʃnz/
Apotheke, Drogerie	—	chemist's /ˈkemɪsts/ (*BrE*), drugstore (*AmE*)
Trafik/Tabakladen	—	tobacconist's /təˈbækənɪsts/
Schallplattenladen	—	record shop
Wein- und Spirituosenhandlung	—	off-licence /ˈɒflaɪsns/
Möbelhaus	—	furniture shop
Sportgeschäft	—	sports shop
Spielwarengeschäft	—	toy shop
Musikalienhandlung	—	music shop
Frisiersalon	—	hairdresser's
Porzellanladen	—	china shop
Geschenkladen	—	gift shop
Reinigung	—	dry cleaner's
Waschsalon	—	launderette /ˌlɔːndəˈret/
Souvenirladen	—	souvenir shop
Großmarkt	—	hypermarket

Shopping

- Can I help you?
- Are you being served?
- I would like a/some ..., please.
- I'm looking for ...
- Can/Could I have ..., please?
- Do you sell ...?
- Excuse me, please, have you got ...?
- I'm just looking, thank you.
- What size do you take?
- I take size ...
- Can I try it/them on?
- Where's the fitting room?
- How much is/are ...?
- I'm sorry, we've sold out/it's sold out/they're sold out.

- I'm afraid we've run out of it.
- It's too expensive.
- I'll take it/them.
- Can I have a carrier bag, please?

- Could I have a receipt, please?

Shopping

Dialogue 1

(Buying clothes)

A   Good morning. Are you being served?

B   No, I'm not. My mother bought me this sweater yesterday. May I change it for a bigger one?

A   Yes, of course. Can I have the receipt, please?

B   Here you are. Do you have a green one?

A   I'm afraid this sweater only comes in two colours, red and black.

B   Then I'd like to try a red one on, please. Where's the fitting room?

A   It's over there, in the corner.

B   Thank you.

B   This size fits perfectly!

A   Good. Anything else?

B   Do you still have any T-shirts at a reduced price?

A   I'm sorry, but we've sold out.

B   What a shame! OK, bye then.

A   Goodbye.

Shopping

Dialogue 2

(At the stationer's)

A   Can I help you?

B   I'm just looking, thank you.

B   How much are the scrapbooks?

A   The small ones are £2.50 and the big ones £5.75.

B   I'd like a small one, please.

A   Anything else?

B   Yes, two calligraphy pens, please.

A   That'll be £5.50.

B   Here's a ten-pound-note.

A   Thank you. £4.50 change.

B   Do you sell video cassettes as well?

A   I'm afraid we don't, but there's a record shop in Albion Road.

B   Thanks. I'll have a look there then. Bye.

A   Bye.

Shopping

(Im Zeitungsgeschäft)

A Guten Morgen.

B Guten Morgen. Was kann ich für Sie tun?

A Den Guardian und zwei Marsriegel, bitte.

B Sonst noch etwas?

A Haben Sie irgendwelche Halspastillen?

B Ja, haben wir.

A Welche Geschmacksrichtungen haben Sie?

B Zitrone & Honig und Eukalyptus.

A Ich nehme die mit Zitrone & Honig.

B Das macht £2.65.

A Hier, bitte.

B Danke. Auf Wiedersehen!

A Auf Wiedersehen!

A *Good morning.*

B *Good morning. What would you like?*

A *The Guardian and two Mars bars, please.*

B *Anything else?*

A *Do you have any throat lozenges?*

B *Yes, we have.*

A *What flavours do you have?*

B *Lemon & honey and eucalyptus.*

A *I'll have the lemon & honey ones, please.*

B *That'll be £2.65.*

A *Here you are.*

B *Thank you. Goodbye.*

A *Bye.*

Shopping

(Im Kleidergeschäft)

A Grüßen Sie und fragen Sie, womit Sie helfen können.

B Sagen Sie, dass Sie ein Hemd (eine Bluse) kaufen möchten.

A Sagen Sie, dass Sie A zeigen werden, welche Hemden Sie haben.

B Bedanken Sie sich.

A Fragen Sie B, welche Farbe es sein soll.

B Nennen Sie eine Farbe.

A Fragen Sie B, welche Größe sie hat.

B Nennen Sie Ihre Kleidergröße.

A Zeigen Sie einige Hemden und fragen Sie, wie sie B gefallen.

B Wählen Sie eines aus und sagen Sie, dass Sie es probieren möchten.

A Erklären Sie, wo sich die Umkleidekabine befindet.

B Kommen Sie zurück und sagen Sie, dass das Hemd passt und Sie es kaufen möchten.

A Nennen Sie den Preis.

B Bezahlen Sie und verabschieden Sie sich.

A Verabschieden Sie sich.

Shopping

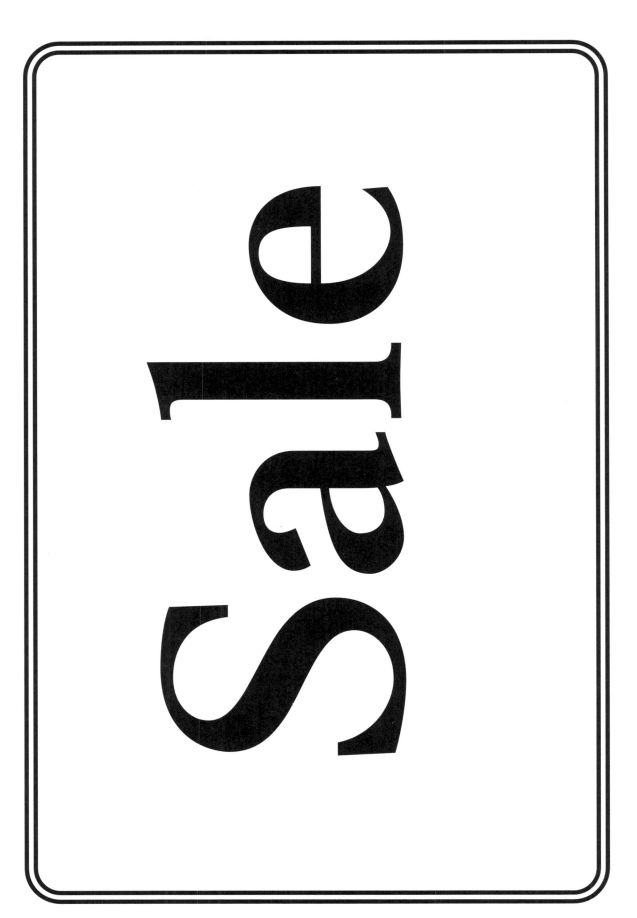

Shopping

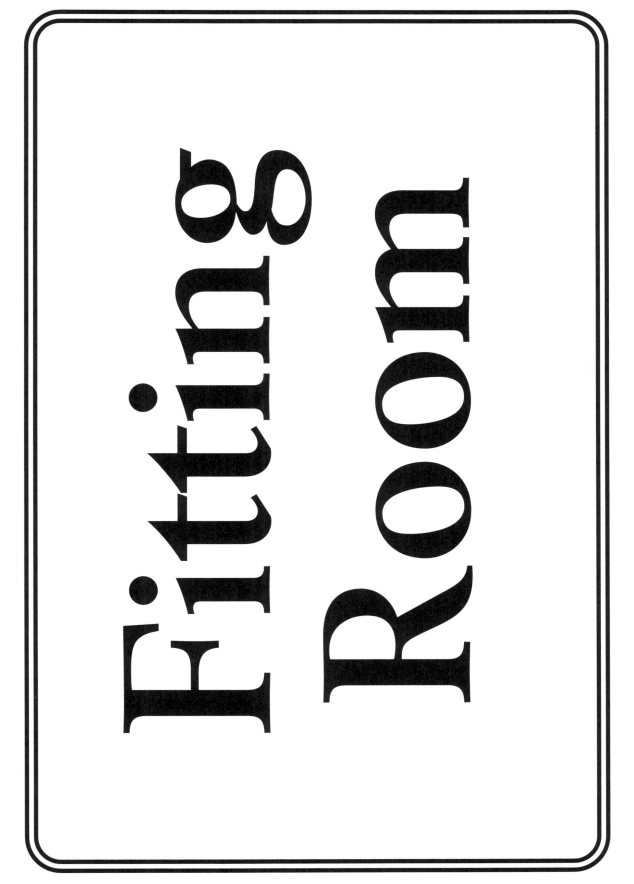

Shopping

Role Cards

When you are about to pay, you realize you've left your purse behind.	When you have paid and are on your way out, the handles on your carrier bag come off.
In the shop you walk straight into a pile of cans. They all fall on the floor.	Unintentionally you happen to break an expensive vase in a gift shop.
When you're queueing to pay you drop your handbag. All your things fall on the floor.	You've brought your little puppy into a shop. Suddenly you notice that it has wet the floor.

Shopping

Role Cards

You are trying on an expensive ring at the jeweller's. After a while you realize it has got stuck.	You're in the fitting room trying some trousers on. Suddenly the zip breaks.
By mistake you walk straight into a huge mirror at the back of the shop.	The cashier says they don't take credit cards. You don't have any cash, but you really want to buy the item in question.
You are given the wrong change, but the shop assistant doesn't believe you.	You want to buy a special thing for your grandfather, but they've sold out.

Shopping

Test Paper

Express yourself in good English.

(Im Warenhaus)

A Sagen Sie, dass Sie eine Jacke probieren möchten.

B Antworten Sie: „Bitte, gerne."

A Fragen Sie, wo die Umkleidekabine ist.

B Antworten Sie: „Da drüben!"

A Fragen Sie, ob es eine kleinere Größe gibt.

B Bejahen Sie.

A Sagen Sie, dass Ihnen die Jacke gefällt, und fragen Sie nach dem Preis.

B Sagen Sie, dass sie £155 kostet.

A Sagen Sie, dass Sie das teuer finden, die Jacke aber dennoch kaufen wollen.

B Fragen Sie, ob A eine Tragetasche möchte.

A Sagen Sie: „Nein danke." Sie möchten die Jacke gleich anziehen.

Shopping

B Fragen Sie, ob A noch etwas anders möchte.

A Sagen Sie: „Nein danke."

B Fragen Sie A, wie sie bezahlen möchte. Mit Scheck, Kreditkarte oder bar?

A Sagen Sie, dass Sie bar bezahlen möchten.

B Wiederholen Sie den Preis.

A Bezahlen Sie. (Was sagen Sie beim Überreichen des Geldes?)

B Bedanken und verabschieden Sie sich.

A Verabschieden Sie sich.

Eating Out

Restaurant	—	restaurant
Gaststätte, -haus	—	inn
einen Tisch bestellen	—	book a table, reserve a table
Teller	—	plate
Glas	—	glass
kleiner Teller	—	small plate
Tasse	—	cup
Untertasse	—	saucer /ˈsɔːsə/
Teelöffel	—	teaspoon
Messer	—	knife
Löffel	—	spoon
Gabel	—	fork
Tischtuch	—	tablecloth
Serviette	—	napkin
Tablett	—	tray
Speisekarte	—	menu /ˈmenjuː/
à la carte/ auf Bestellung	—	à la carte /ˌɑː lɑː ˈkɑːt/
Menü/Tagesgericht	—	set menu
Tagesempfehlung	—	today's special
schmackhaft	—	tasty
saftig	—	juicy
Spezialität	—	speciality /ˌspeʃiˈæləti/
bestellen	—	order
Rechnung	—	bill
Mehrwertsteuer inklusive	—	VAT (value-added tax) included
Bedienung inklusive	—	service included
Trinkgeld	—	tip
Kellner	—	waiter
Kellnerin	—	waitress
Gericht	—	dish

Eating Out

Vorspeise	—	starter
Hauptgericht	—	main course
Dessert, Nachtisch	—	dessert /dɪˈzɜːt/, sweet
Gemüse	—	vegetables /ˈvedʒtəblz/
Getränke	—	drinks, beverages /ˈbevrɪdʒɪz/
Ich bin satt, ich kann nicht mehr	—	I've had enough to eat, I simply couldn't eat any more, I'm full (up)
Kaffee/Tee mit/ohne Milch	—	black/white coffee/tea

Eating Out

Food

Schweinefleisch	—	pork
Rindfleisch	—	beef
Kalbfleisch	—	veal /viːl/
Lamm	—	lamb
Schinken	—	ham
Leber	—	liver /ˈlɪvə/
Roastbeef	—	roast beef
Wurst	—	sausage /ˈsɒsɪdʒ/
Huhn	—	chicken
Truthahn	—	turkey
gut durchgebraten	—	well done
blutig	—	rare /reə/
medium/halb durchgebraten	—	medium
Kartoffel	—	potato
Pommes frites	—	chips, French fries
Kartoffelpüree	—	mashed potatoes, mash
gebackene Kartoffel	—	jacket /ˈdʒækɪt/ potato, baked potato
Shrimps	—	shrimps
Garnele	—	prawn
Krabbe	—	crab
Kabeljau/Dorsch	—	cod
Scholle	—	plaice /pleɪs/
Lachs	—	salmon /ˈsæmən/
Forelle	—	trout
Flussbarsch	—	perch /pɜːtʃ/
Hecht	—	pike
Makrele	—	mackerel /ˈmækrəl/
Gurke	—	cucumber /ˈkjuːkʌmbə/
Karotte	—	carrot
Tomate	—	tomato

Eating Out

Häuptel-/Kopfsalat	—	lettuce /ˈletɪs/
Salat	—	salad
Karfiol/Blumenkohl	—	cauliflower /ˈkɒliflaʊə/
Erbsen	—	peas
Zwiebel	—	onion /ˈʌnjən/
Knoblauch	—	garlic
Bohnen	—	beans
Paprika	—	pepper
Pilz	—	mushroom /ˈmʌʃrʊm/
Porree/Lauch	—	leek
Kohlsprossen/ Rosenkohl	—	Brussels sprouts /ˌbrʌslz ˈspraʊts/ *(pl.)*

Eating Out

- Could I have the menu, please?

- Waiter, we/I would like to order, please.

- Can I take your order?

- What would you like?

- What would you like as a starter?

- What would you like to follow?

- What would you like for your main course?

- Would you like a dessert?

- Anything to drink?
- I would like a …
- I'll have my steak rare/medium/well done, please.

- Could I have the bill, please?

- Is service included?

Eating Out

YOUTH PUB
Samstag 6. Januar
Open House
ab 20 Uhr
Music, Fun, Talk, Snack
Special:
Gäste aus Costa Rica, England, Irland, Kanada, Ukraine und USA;
RC./ Dr. Külz-Str. 21; gegenüber Wohnheim Ingenieurschule

... and mixed grill to ...

... ter and a glass of red wine, ...

A ... ks in a minute.

B Thank you.

B Waiter, can I have the bill, please?

A Certainly.

B Service is included, isn't it?

A Yes, it is. Here's your change, sir, £1.25.

B Keep it!

A Thank you very much, sir! Goodbye.

B Goodbye.

Eating Out

Dialogue 2

A Can I have the menu, please?

B Certainly. Do you want to order straight away?

A Yes, please. I'll have veal and ham pie and a mixed salad, please.

B Anything to drink?

A I'd like half a lager, please.

B Is everything all right for you?

A Yes, thank you. The pie was very tasty!

B Thank you. Would you like a dessert?

A Yes, please. What have you got?

B We've got mixed ice cream, fruit salad and chocolate cake.

A I'll have chocolate cake and a black coffee, please. And could I have the bill straight away? I'm in a bit of a hurry.

B Of course, just a minute.

A Thank you.

Eating Out

(Das Telefon läutet.)

A Cranes Restaurant. Was kann ich für Sie tun?

B Hallo! Ich möchte gerne für heute Abend um 19.30 Uhr einen Tisch bestellen.

A ...

B ...

A ...

B ...

A ...

B ...

A Auf Wiederhören! Wir freuen uns auf Ihren Besuch heute Abend!

A *Good afternoon. Crane's restaurant. Can I help you?*

B *Hello! I'd like to book a table for this evening at 7.30.*

A *...tainly! For how ...eople?*

B *...r.*

A *...t name, please?*

B *...me is Meier.*

A *...ing or non-smoking?*

B *...smoking, please. ...ve have a table by ...indow, please?*

A *...of course.*

B *...k you very much. ...dbye.*

A *Goodbye. We look forward to seeing you this evening.*

YOUTH PUB

Samstag 6. Januar
Open House

ab 20 Uhr

Music, Fun, Talk, Snack

Special:

Gäste aus Costa Rica, England, Irland, Kanada, Ukraine und USA;

RC./ Dr. Külz-Str. 21: gegenüber Wohnheim Ingenieurschule

Eating Out

A Grüßen Sie und sagen Sie, dass Sie gerne essen möchten.

→ B Sagen Sie: „Ja, gerne", und fragen Sie A, ob sie à la carte essen oder die Tageskarte haben möchte.

A Sagen Sie, dass Sie die Tageskarte haben möchten.

→ B Geben Sie A diese Karte und sagen Sie, dass Sie gleich zurückkommen werden.

A Danken Sie.

→ B Fragen Sie, ob A bereit für die Bestellung ist.

A Bejahen Sie und sagen Sie, welche Vorspeise und welches Hauptgericht Sie gewählt haben.

→ B Fragen Sie, was A zu trinken haben möchte.

A Antworten Sie darauf.

B Fragen Sie, ob A eine Nachspeise haben möchte.

A Lehnen Sie dankend ab und sagen Sie, dass Sie zahlen möchten.

→ B Nennen Sie den Rechnungsbetrag.

A Überreichen Sie den Betrag mit einem kleinen Trinkgeld.

→ B Bedanken und verabschieden Sie sich.

A Verabschieden Sie sich.

Menu

Starters

Soup of the day £1.50
Grapefruit 90p
Prawn cocktail £2.25

Main Courses

Veal & ham pie £3.80
Mixed grill & chips £5.00
Roast beef & Yorkshire pudding £5.25
Plaice & chips £4.25

Vegetables

Mixed salad £1.50
Carrots £1.00
Cauliflower.........................£1.00

Desserts

Fruit salad..........................£2.00
Mixed ice cream £1.50
Cheese & biscuits £2.85

Beverages

Coke, Sprite, Mineral water 95p
Milk, Orange juice 80p
Coffee, Tea, Cocoa £1.25

Eating Out

The Bull and Dragon

Lunch

served from 11.30 am till 2.45 pm

Soup of the day
Tomato juice
Mixed salad

Trout
Smoked salmon
Roast chicken
Pork chops

Peas
Brussels sprouts
French fried potatoes

Banana split
Chocolate gateau
Fruit cocktail

Coffee

Price: £6.45   (incl. VAT)

Eating Out

Role Cards

You have left your money at home.	The waiter brings you the wrong food.
You are given the wrong change.	The waiter drops something on you.
Your food isn't hot enough.	Your food is burnt.
You get a dirty plate.	There is an insect in your soup.

Eating Out

Role Cards

The waitress spills some coffee on your new sweater.	You happen to spill your glass of coke on the table.
You don't have enough money to pay the bill.	You asked for a white coffee, but get a black one with sugar, which you hate.
You've booked a table for five, but the reservation is for only two people.	You've booked a table at 8.30 pm but arrive at the restaurant at 8.55 pm.

Eating Out

Test Paper

Express yourself in good English.

(Im Restaurant)

A   Bitten Sie um die Speisekarte.

B   Sagen Sie: „Bitte sehr!"

B   Fragen Sie den Gast, ob Sie schon die Bestellung aufnehmen können.

A   Antworten Sie mit Ja und sagen Sie, dass Sie eine Vorspeise bestellen möchten. Sagen Sie, welche Vorspeise Sie wünschen.

B   Fragen Sie, ob sie ein Hauptgericht bestellen möchte.

A   Bejahen Sie und sagen Sie, was Sie bestellen möchten.

B   Fragen Sie, ob sie auch eine Nachspeise haben möchte.

Eating Out

A Lehnen Sie dankend ab und sagen Sie, dass Sie aber gerne etwas zu trinken hätten.

B Sagen Sie, aus welchen Getränken gewählt werden kann.

A Bestellen Sie eines der Getränke.

A Bitten Sie um die Rechnung.

B Geben Sie A die Rechnung und nennen Sie den Rechnungsbetrag.

A Fragen Sie, ob das Trinkgeld inkludiert ist.

B Antworten Sie mit Ja.

A Geben Sie der KellnerIn das Geld und sagen Sie: „Bitte sehr, hier sind …" (Nennen Sie den Betrag.)

B Bedanken Sie sich.

A Bedanken und verabschieden Sie sich.

B Verabschieden Sie sich.

Being Ill

Arzt, Ärztin	—	doctor
Krankenschwester	—	nurse
Krankenhaus	—	hospital
Ordination	—	surgery /ˈsɜːdʒəri/
Ordinationszeiten	—	surgery hours (*pl.*)
Ärztezentrum	—	medical/health centre
Unfallstation	—	emergency ward /ɪˈmɜːdʒənsi wɔːd/
Station (Krankenhaus)	—	ward, unit
Apotheke	—	chemist's /ˈkemɪsts/ (*BrE*), drugstore (*AmE*)
Arznei	—	medicine
Rezept	—	prescription
krankgeschrieben sein	—	be on sick leave
Krankheit	—	illness, disease /dɪˈziːz/
Doktordiplom	—	doctor's certificate /səˈtɪfɪkət/
ärztliche Untersuchung	—	medical examination
Krankenwagen	—	ambulance
einen Term vereinbaren	—	make an appointment
krank sein	—	be ill/sick
Rückenschmerzen haben	—	have backache
Ohrenschmerzen haben	—	have earache
Kopfschmerzen haben	—	have a headache /ˈhedeɪk/
Halsschmerzen haben	—	have a sore throat
Fieber haben	—	have a temperature
Hautausschlag haben	—	have a rash /ræʃ/
Meine Nase ist verstopft	—	I have a blocked nose, my nose is/feels blocked
Grippe haben	—	have flu (influenza)
Magenschmerzen haben	—	have stomachache /ˈstʌməkeɪk/
ich habe mir den Magen verdorben	—	my stomach /ˈstʌmək/ is upset
Husten haben	—	have a cough /kɒf/

Being III

erkältet sein	—	have a cold
Sonnenbrand haben	—	have got sunburnt
Schmerz(en)	—	ache, pain
sich übergeben, erbrechen	—	be sick, vomit /ˈvɒmɪt/, throw up (*informell*)
Wunde	—	wound /wuːnd/
Schnittwunde/ klaffende Wunde	—	cut, gash (= lang und tief)
sich den Knöchel verstauchen	—	sprain one's ankle
allergisch sein gegen	—	be allergic to /əˈlɜːdʒɪk/
Asthma haben	—	be asthmatic /æsˈmætɪk/
schwindlig	—	dizzy
Papiertaschentücher	—	paper handkerchiefs /ˈhæŋkətʃɪfs/, hankies /ˈhæŋkiz/ (*informell*), tissues /ˈtɪʃuːz/
Watte	—	cotton wool
Lutschtabletten, Halspastillen	—	throat lozenges /ˈθrəʊt ˌlɒzɪndʒɪz/
Hustensaft	—	cough mixture
Aspirin	—	aspirin(s)
Tablette	—	pill, tablet
Salbe	—	ointment /ˈɔɪntmənt/, cream
Verband	—	bandage /ˈbændɪdʒ/
Sonnenöl, -creme	—	suntan lotion
Desinfektionsmittel	—	disinfectant
Thermometer	—	thermometer /θəˈmɒmɪtə/
Pflaster	—	plaster
eingipsen	—	put in plaster
Vitamintabletten	—	vitamin tablets

Being III

Parts of the Body

Kopf	—	head
Stirn	—	forehead /ˈfɒrɪd/
Ohr	—	ear
Auge	—	eye
Nase	—	nose
Kinn	—	chin
Kiefer	—	jaw /dʒɔː/
Backe, Wange	—	cheek
Mund	—	mouth
Lippe	—	lip
Zahn	—	tooth (*pl.* teeth)
Hals	—	neck
Hals, Rachen	—	throat /θrəʊt/
Hinterkopf	—	back of the head
Schulter	—	shoulder
Brustkorb	—	chest
Brust	—	breast /brest/
Rücken	—	back
Taille	—	waist
Magen	—	stomach /ˈstʌmək/
Arm	—	arm
Ellbogen	—	elbow
Handgelenk	—	wrist /rɪst/
Hand	—	hand
Finger	—	finger
Daumen	—	thumb /θʌm/
Handfläche	—	palm /pɑːm/
Hüfte	—	hip
Gesäßbacke	—	buttock /ˈbʌtək/
Gesäß	—	behind, bottom
Bein	—	leg
(Ober)Schenkel	—	thigh /θaɪ/

Being III

Knie	—	knee /niː/
Kniescheibe	—	kneecap
Wade	—	calf (*pl.* calves)
Knöchel	—	ankle
Fuß	—	foot (*pl.* feet)
Zehe	—	toe
Ferse	—	heel

Being III

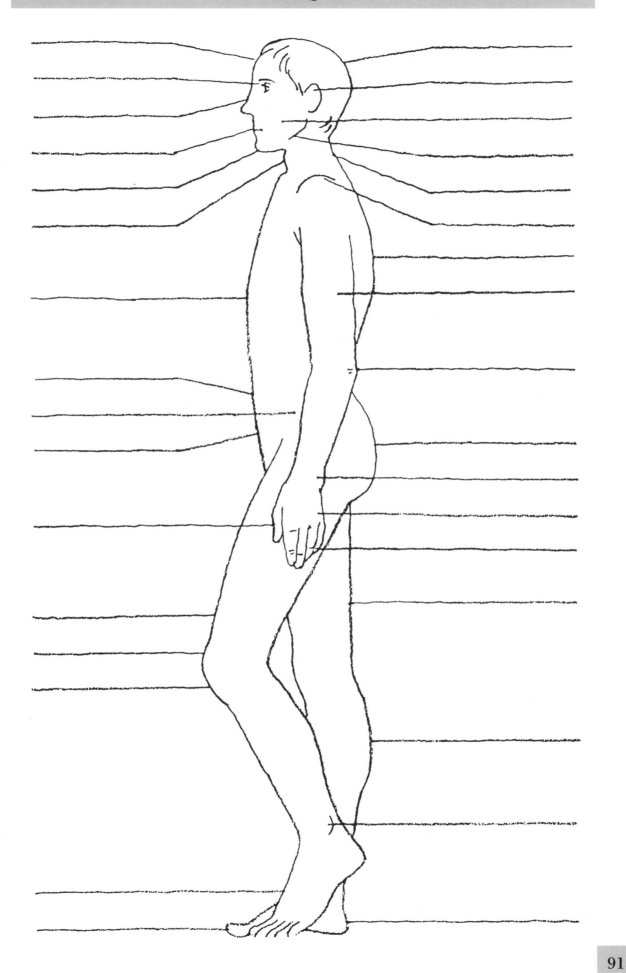

Being Ill

- How are you?
- What's the matter/problem?
- What seems to be the trouble?

- I'm fine, thank you.
- I'm quite all right, thank you.

- I'm not feeling very well.

- I need to see a doctor.

- I'd like to make an appointment.

- Excuse me, can you tell me if there's a chemist's nearby?

- I have a cold. What can I get for it?

- You can only buy this medicine on prescription.

- You must dissolve these pills in water.

Being Ill

Dialogue 1

(At the chemist's)

A Good morning.

B Good morning. Can I help you?

A Yes, please. I'm not feeling very well.

B What's wrong?

A I have a headache.

B You need some aspirin. Would you like a large or a small bottle?

A A small one, please.

B Here you are.

A Thanks. I also need something for my grandmother. She's had a bad cough for quite a few days now.

B Try some cough mixture. Three spoonfuls twice a day. And if she doesn't get better in a week, advise her to see a doctor.

A I will. How much do I owe you?

B £2.50 for the aspirins and £3.25 for the cough mixture. £5.75 in all.

A Here's a ten-pound-note.

B Thank you. £4.25 for you.

A Thank you. Goodbye.

B Goodbye.

Being III

Dialogue 2

(The phone is ringing.)

A   Dr Smith's surgery. Can I help you?

B   Good morning. My name is David Baxter. I'd like to make an appointment to see the doctor.

A   Would 2.30 this afternoon suit you?

B   Yes, that would be fine.

A   Good. I'll put you down for 2.30 pm then.

B   Thank you very much.

A   Thank you. Goodbye.

B   Bye.

(2.30 pm at the surgery)

C   Good afternoon. What seems to be the trouble?

B   I've got a sore throat and a temperature, and ever since I woke up this morning I've been feeling dizzy.

C   It sounds as if you've got a nasty cold. Go down to the chemist's and get yourself some aspirin and throat lozenges. You won't need a prescription for that.

B   Thank you. Goodbye.

C   Goodbye.

Being Ill

(Das Telefon läutet.)

A   Ordination Dr. Bartley, guten Morgen!

B   Guten Morgen. Ich möchte gerne einen Termin bei Dr. Bartley.

A   Einen Moment, bitte, ich muss in den Kalender schauen. /.../ Passt Ihnen morgen, 14.15 Uhr?

B   Das ist leider zu spät. Wie wär's mit übermorgen?

A   Ich könnte Sie um 9.00 Uhr morgens einschieben.

B   Das wäre gut.

A   Gut. Wie ist Ihr Name, bitte?

B   Deacon.

A   OK, Frau/Herr Deacon. Übermorgen um 9.00 Uhr.

B   Vielen Dank. Auf Wiederhören!

A   Auf Wiederhören!

A   *Good morning. Dr Bartley's surgery.*

B   *Good morning. I'd like to make an appointment with Dr Bartley.*

A   *Hold on, please. I'll have a look in the diary. /.../ Is 2.15 tomorrow all right?*

B   *I'm afraid it's too late. What about the day after tomorrow?*

A   *I could fit you in at 9.00 in the morning.*

B   *That would be fine.*

A   *Good. Your name, Sir/Madam?*

B   *Deacon.*

A   *OK, Mrs/Mr Deacon. 9 am the day after tomorrow.*

B   *Thank you very much. Goodbye.*

A   *Goodbye.*

Being III

(In der Apotheke)

A Grüßen Sie und fragen Sie, womit Sie dienen können.

B Sagen Sie, dass Sie sich nicht wohl fühlen, dass Sie Kopf- und Halsschmerzen haben.

A Fragen Sie, ob B auch Fieber hat.

B Sagen Sie, dass Sie das nicht annehmen.

A Sagen Sie, dass Sie glauben, B habe eine Erkältung.

B Fragen Sie, ob Sie etwas dagegen haben können.

A Schlagen Sie Lutschtabletten und Aspirin vor.

B Sagen Sie, dass Sie damit einverstanden sind. Bitten Sie um eine kleine Packung Aspirin. Fragen Sie, was sie kostet.

A Sagen Sie den Betrag.

B Bezahlen Sie den genauen Preis.

A Danken Sie und wünschen Sie gute Besserung.

B Bedanken und verabschieden Sie sich.

A Verabschieden Sie sich.

Being Ill

Role Cards

a headache	a sore throat
a high temperature	a blocked nose
flu	a cough
a cold	sunburn
stomachache	a rash

Being Ill

Role Cards

throat lozenges	aspirin
a bottle of pills	cream
handkerchiefs	suntan lotion
cough mixture	thermometer
ointment	vitamins

Being III

Test Paper

Express yourself in good English.

(In der Apotheke)

A Grüßen Sie.

B Grüßen Sie und fragen Sie, womit Sie behilflich sein können.

A Sagen Sie, dass Sie sich nicht wohl fühlen.

B Fragen Sie, was A fehlt.

A Sagen Sie, dass Sie glauben, eine Erkältung zu haben.

B Fragen Sie, ob A schon beim Arzt gewesen ist.

A Sagen Sie, dass Sie nicht glauben, dass das notwendig ist, da Sie nur Kopf- und Halsschmerzen haben.

B Schlagen Sie A vor, Lutschtabletten und eine Packung Aspirin zu kaufen. Sagen Sie, dass das rezeptfrei erhältlich ist.

Being III

A Sagen Sie, dass Sie das gut finden. Fragen Sie, was das kostet.

B Nenen Sie den Preis.

A Bezahlen Sie.

B Geben Sie A das Wechselgeld und die Arzneien.

A Bedanken und verabschieden Sie sich.

B Verabschieden Sie sich.

At the Railway Station

Bahnhof	—	railway station
Zug	—	train
Schnellzug, Direktzug	—	through train, express train
Güterzug	—	goods train
Lok	—	engine /ˈendʒin/
Waggon	—	railway carriage /ˈkærɪdʒ/
Abteil	—	compartment
Speisewagen	—	dining-car, restaurant-car
Buffetwagen	—	buffet /ˈbʊfeɪ/ car
Schlafwagen	—	sleeping-car
Liegewagen	—	couchette /kuːˈʃet/
Bahnsteig	—	platform
Gleis	—	railway track
Bahnreise	—	train journey /ˈdʒɜːni/
Fahrplan	—	timetable
Fahrkarte	—	ticket
Fahrkartenschalter	—	ticket office
einfache Fahrkarte	—	single ticket
Rückfahrkarte	—	return ticket
Tagesrückfahrkarte	—	day return ticket
Platzkarte	—	seat reservation (ticket)
Fahrkartenautomat	—	(automatic) ticket machine
Bahnsteigkarte	—	platform ticket
Auskunftsschalter	—	information counter
Wartesaal	—	waiting room
SchaffnerIn	—	ticket-collector, guard
Fahrgast	—	passenger
umsteigen	—	change trains
Gepäckaufbewahrung	—	left-luggage office
Gepäckschließfach	—	left-luggage locker
Fundbüro	—	lost property office
Eisenbahnverbindung	—	rail service
Bahnknotenpunkt	—	junction /ˈdʒʌŋkʃən/

At the Railway Station

Bahnübergang — level crossing
Schranken — barrier

At the Railway Station

- Excuse me, please. How do I get to the railway station from here?

- How much is a single/return ticket to Glasgow, please?

- A single to Penzance, please.

- Can I have a day return to Birmingham, please?

- Do I have to reserve a seat?

- When is the next train to London?

- Which platform does it leave from?

- Do I have to change trains?
- When does it get to Crawley?

- How long does it take?
- Is there a buffet car on this train?

At the Railway Station

Dialogue 1

(At the ticket office)

A Good morning.

B Good morning.

A I'd like a return ticket to London, please.

B Are you coming back today?

A Yes, around ten o'clock tonight.

B Would you like a cheap day return?

A What's the difference?

B Well, an ordinary return ticket is £6.50, whereas a day return only costs £4.75.

A I see. Thanks for telling me. I'll have a day return then.

B That'll be £4.75.

A When is the next train to London?

B There's one in about 15 minutes. Then there's an intercity train at 8.45. It's much faster.

A From which platform?

B Let me see … platform 10.

A Thank you. Goodbye.

B Bye. Have a nice journey!

At the Railway Station

Dialogue 2

(In the street)

A   Excuse me, could you please tell me the way to the railway station?

B   It's just around the corner.

A   Thank you.

(At the ticket office)

A   Hello, I'd like a single to Brighton, please.

C   First or second class?

A   Second class, please.

C   That'll be £8.95.

A   Here's £10. Do I have to change trains?

C   Yes, I'm afraid you'll have to change at Burgess Hill.

A   When is the next train?

C   Well, there's one in about half an hour, at 10.15.

A   Which platform does it go from?

C   Platform 2.

A   Thank you.

C   Don't forget your

A   Oh, thanks! Bye.

C   Bye.

At the Railway Station

(Am Fahrkartenschalter)

A   Guten Morgen. Kann ich eine Fahrkarte nach Southampton haben, bitte?

B   Eine einfache oder eine Rückfahrkarte?

A   Eine Rückfahrkarte, bitte.

B   Das macht £12.65.

A   Wann fahren die Züge nach Southampton?

B   Zu jeder vollen Stunde.

A   Gibt es einen Direktzug?

B   Nein, Sie müssen in Basingstoke umsteigen.

A   Auf welchem Bahnsteig fährt der Zug ab?

B   Bahnsteig 3.

A   Danke.

A   *Good morning. Can I have a ticket to Southampton, please?*

B   *Single or return?*

A   *Return, please.*

B   *That'll be £12.65, please.*

A   *What are the times of the trains to Southampton?*

B   *There is a train every hour on the hour.*

A   *Is it a through train?*

B   *No, you change at Basingstoke.*

A   *Which platform does it go from?*

B   *Platform 3.*

A   *Thank you.*

At the Railway Station

(Am Fahrkartenschalter)

A   Bitten Sie um eine Retourfahrkarte nach Oxford.

  B   Fragen Sie, ob A am selben Tag zurückfahren wird.

A   Sagen Sie, dass Sie das ganze Wochenende bleiben werden.

  B   Fragen Sie, ob die Fahrkarte für die 1. oder 2. Klasse sein soll.

A   Antworten Sie, dass Sie eine Fahrkarte 1. Klasse haben möchten, und fragen Sie, ob Sie umsteigen müssen.

  B   Sagen Sie, dass A in Reading umsteigen muss.

A   Fragen Sie, ob Sie eine Platzreservierung brauchen.

  B   Antworten Sie, das dass nicht notwendig ist.

A   Fragen Sie, wie lange die Fahrt nach Oxford dauert.

  B   Sagen Sie, das Sie ca. 1 Stunde und 15 Minuten dauert.

A   Fragen Sie, wann und auf welchem Bahnsteig der nächste Zug abfährt.

  B   Nennen Sie Zeit und Bahnsteignummer.

A   Bedanken und verabschieden Sie sich.

  B   Verabschieden Sie sich.

At the Railway Station

Tickets and Information

At the Railway Station

Eastbourne and Polegate to London

		🎩	MX	🎩	🎩	FX
Eastbourne	06.26	07.32	08.33	09.00	then every hour on the hour until 21.00	22.35
Hampden Park	06.29	07.18B	08.16B	08.49B		22.39
Polegate	06.35	07.39	08.40	09.06		22.43
Lewes	06.52	—	08.59	09.21		23.02
East Croydon	07.47	08.46	09.59	10.10		00.22f
London Bridge	08.03	—	10.15d	10.30d		00.51f
London Victoria	08.10d	09.05	10.09	10.29		00.57g

Through trains are shown in bold type. Connecting services are in light type.

At the Railway Station

London to Polegate and Eastbourne

	🎩	C	FX	🎩	
London Victoria	06.47	17.16	18.16	19.47	then at
London Bridge	06.20d	then at	17.12d	18.15e	19.43d	the same
East Croydon	07.03	the same	17.33	18.33	20.03	minutes
Lewes	07.53	minutes	18.19	19.25	20.52	past each
Polegate	08.07	past each	18.39	19.41	21.06	hour until
Hampden Park	08.12	hour until	18.44	19.46	21.22A	22.47
Eastbourne	08.16	15.47	18.51	19.52	21.13	

Through trains are shown in bold type. Connecting services are in light type.

Kopiervorlage • Excuse me, please ... ISBN 3-7058-5557-3
©VERITAS-Verlag

At the Railway Station

Eastbourne to London Train Times

Notes:

A   Calls at Hampden Park after Eastbourne

B   Calls at Hampden Park before Eastbourne

C   Train divides en route. Please travel in rear part of train.

d   Change at East Croydon

e   Change at Haywards Heath

f   Change at Brighton

g   Change at Brighton and East Croydon

FX Fridays excepted

MX Mondays excepted

☕ Buffet Service available for all or part of journey.

At the Railway Station

Penalty Fares

Penalty Fares are in operation at all stations and on all trains within Network SouthCentral. Please ensure you have a valid ticket before travelling.

At the Railway Station

Safety Messsage

For your own safety and those on the platform, please do not open the doors until the train has stopped.

At the Railway Station

Role Cards (easy)

You want a return ticket from Eastbourne to London Victoria.	You're in Eastbourne and want to know if there is a train to London late in the evening.
You want to know which platform the next train to Polegate goes from.	You're in Polegate and want to go to London for the day. Ask for a cheap day return ticket.
You're going to London from Lewes. The train leaves at 09.21. You want to know if you can get anything to eat on the train.	You're going to London from Polegate at 07.39. You want to know if you have to change trains.

At the Railway Station

Role Cards (easy)

You want to know how long it takes to get to London Victoria from Eastbourne.	You're in Eastbourne and want to know how often the trains leave for East Croydon in the afternoon.
You're in Eastbourne and want a single ticket to London Bridge.	You're going on the 9 o'clock train from Eastbourne to Polegate. Ask what time the train gets there.
You're going to London Victoria from Polegate on a Monday morning. You have to be there before 10.15. Ask what time the train goes.	You're in Hampden Park and want to know if there is an early morning train to East Croydon.

At the Railway Station

Role Cards

You're in Eastbourne and want to go to London on an early morning train. You don't want to change trains. You would like something to eat on the train.	You're in Eastbourne and want to go to East Croydon during the afternoon the following day. Find out how often the trains leave.
You want a cheap day return ticket from Polegate to London. Find out what time the trains go to Polegate in the evening.	It's 8 o'clock in the morning. You're at London Bridge Station and want to know when the next train to Polegate goes. Buy a single ticket.

At the Railway Station

Role Cards

You're going to Eastbourne from London Victoria at 17.16. You want to know if you need a seat reservation, or if you can sit anywhere you like.	You want to go to Hampden Park from East Croydon after work on a Friday afternoon. You also want to know how long it takes.
You're on holiday in Eastbourne and would like to spend the weekend in London. Find out when the trains go on Fridays and Sundays. Buy tickets.	It's 06.30 on a Monday morning. You've just missed the train from Eastbourne to London Bridge. You have a very important meeting at 10.00. Find out if there's another train. Buy another ticket.

At the Railway Station

Test Paper

Express yourself in good English.

(Am Bahnhof)

A   Fragen Sie B, wo man Fahrkarten kaufen kann.

B   Sagen Sie, dass sich der Fahrkartenschalter gegenüber dem Wartesaal befindet.

A   Danken Sie.

(Am Fahrkartenschalter)

A   Grüßen Sie und bitten Sie um eine Fahrkarte nach London.

C   Fragen Sie, ob A eine einfache oder eine Retourfahrkarte haben möchte.

A   Sagen Sie, dass Sie eine Retourfahrkarte haben möchten.

C   Fragen Sie, ob A heute noch zurückfahren wird.

At the Railway Station

A   Antworten Sie: „Ja, am Abend."

C   Schlagen Sie A vor, eine billige Retourfahrkarte mit einem Tag Gültigkeitsdauer zu kaufen.

A   Fragen Sie, was das kostet.

C   Nennen Sie den Preis.

A   Fragen Sie, wann der nächste Zug nach London abfährt.

C   Antworten Sie.

A   Fragen Sie, wie lange die Fahrt dauert und ob Sie umsteigen müssen.

C   Sagen Sie, dass es ein Direktzug ist und dass A nicht umsteigen muss. Sagen Sie, wie lange die Fahrt dauert.

A   Fragen Sie, auf welchem Bahnsteig der Zug abfährt.

C   Antworten Sie.

A   Bedanken und verabschieden Sie sich.

C   Verabschieden Sie sich und wünschen Sie eine angenehme Reise.

Making Telephone Calls

Telefon	—	telephone
Anrufbeantworter	—	answering machine
Telefonzelle	—	telephone box
Telefonkarte	—	phone card
Telefonbuch	—	telephone directory /dəˈrektəri/
Telefonnummer	—	(telephone) number
Vorwahl	—	dialling code (*BrE*), area code (*AmE*)
Landesvorwahl	—	country code
Hörer	—	receiver /rɪˈsiːvə/
eine Nummer wählen	—	dial /ˈdaɪəl/ a number
Telefongespräch	—	(telephone) call
Ortsgespräch	—	local call
Ferngespräch	—	long-distance call
R-Gespräch	—	reverse /rɪˈvɜːs/ charge call (*BrE*), collect call (*AmE*)
telefonieren	—	make a (telephone) call
jemanden anrufen	—	phone/ring a person
ein Telefongespräch entgegennehmen	—	take a call
ans Telefon gehen	—	answer the phone
zurückrufen	—	call back
besetzt	—	engaged (*BrE*), busy (*AmE*)
auflegen	—	hang up
Auskunft	—	directory enquiries /ɪnˈkwaɪəriz/
Telefonzentrale	—	switchboard, telephone exchange
Vermittlung	—	operator

Making Telephone Calls

Nebenanschluss, Durchwahl	—	extension
etwas ausrichten	—	take a message
eine Nachricht hinterlassen	—	leave a message
Amtszeichen	—	dialling tone
Telefonleitung	—	line, connection
Wertkartentelefon	—	cardphone
Mobiltelefon	—	mobile (tele)phone

Making Telephone Calls

- Excuse me, do you know if there's a telephone box nearby?

- Can I have your (telephone) number, please?

- The dialling code/area code for Vienna is 01.

- He's on the (tele)phone.

- There's a call for you. / You're wanted on the (tele)phone.

- I'm sorry, I must have dialled the wrong number.

- Can I speak to …, please? / I'd like to speak to …, please.

- Speaking.
- Hold on, please. / Hold the line, please.
- Can I take a message?
- The number is engaged/busy.

- I'll put you through.(*BrE*) / I'll connect you.(*AmE*)

Making Telephone Calls

Dialogue 1

A 87 29 40.

B Hello. My name is Peter Sutton. Can I speak to Mr Lewis, please?

A I'm afraid he's not in at the moment.

B Oh, when will he be back?

A He said he'd be back tomorrow. Can I take a message?

B Yes, would you let him know I called?

A Of course, what's your name again?

B Sutton. Peter Sutton.

A I'll let him know when he comes in tomorrow.

B Thank you very much. Goodbye.

A Goodbye.

Making Telephone Calls

Dialogue 2

A   66 31 80.

B   Good afternoon. This is John Ross of Mill's Garage. Could I speak to Mr Harrow, please?

A   I'm afraid my husband's not in just now. Would you like to leave a message?

B   Yes. Would you tell him his car is ready, please?

A   Oh, yes. He won't be long. What time do you close?

B   At 4 pm.

A   I'll tell him when he comes in.

B   Thank you. Goodbye.

A   Goodbye.

Telephone Calls

Dialogues

- ... speak to Liz, please?
- ... you.

- ... Wilson, please?

A I'm afraid there's no Mrs Wilson here.

B Isn't this 30 04 73?

A No, it's 30 04 72.

B Oh, I'm terribly sorry. I must have dialled the wrong number.

A That's all right. Goodbye.

B Goodbye.

A Good morning. Collins & Co.

B Good morning. May I speak to the Sales Manager, please?

A Certainly. I'll connect you.

B Thank you.

Making Telephone Calls

Short Dialogues

A Eastbourne College. Good morning.

B Good morning. I'd like to speak to Ms Beck, please.

A I'm afraid she's gone out for lunch. Can I take a message?

B Yes. My name is Lee Parker, from Parker's Book Shop. Could you tell her that we've now got the book she ordered last week?

A Yes, of course, I'll tell her.

B Thank you. Goodbye.

A Directory enquiries. Which name, please?

B George Milford, 108 Chester Terrace, York.

C (*recorded voice*) The number you require is (01904) 88 01 76. I repeat …

A Karen Beck speaking.

B Oh, hello. Is your mother in, Karen? This is Mrs Collins.

A Hold on, Mrs Collins. I'll see if she's in.

Making Telephone Calls

A Vermittlung! Kann ich Ihnen helfen?

B Ich möchte ein R-Gespräch führen.

A Wohin?

B Nach Österreich.

A Welche Nummer?

B Die Vorwahl ist 01, die Nummer ist 703 30 46.

A Ihr Name, bitte.

B Anna Hofer.

A Wen möchten Sie sprechen?

B Frau Hofer.

A Einen Moment, bitte.

C Hofer.

A Frau Hofer, hier ist ein R-Gespräch von Anna Hofer aus Großbritannien. Wollen Sie für das Gespräch bezahlen?

C Ja.

A Gut, übernehmen Sie!

C Vielen Dank!

A *Operator. Can I help you?*

B *I'd like to make a reverse charge call, please.*

A *Where to?*

B *To Austria.*

A *What number?*

B *The dialling code is 01 and the number is 703 30 46.*

A *Your name, please.*

B *Anna Hofer.*

A *Who would you like to speak to?*

B *Mrs Hofer.*

A *Hold on, please.*

C *Hofer.*

A *Mrs Hofer, this is a reverse charge call from Miss Hofer, Great Britain. Will you pay for the call?*

C *Yes.*

A *OK, go ahead.*

C *Thank you very much.*

Making Telephone Calls

(Das Telefon läutet.)

A   Heben Sie ab und nennen Sie Ihre Telefonnummer.

B   Nennen Sie Ihren Namen und fragen Sie, ob Sie Colin sprechen können.

A   Sagen Sie, dass er gerade weggegangen ist, um eine Zeitung zu kaufen.

B   Fragen Sie A, wann sie glaubt, dass Colin zurückkommen wird.

A   Sagen Sie, dass Sie das nicht wissen, dass es aber wahrscheinlich nicht lange dauert.

B   Fragen Sie, ob Sie eine Mitteilung hinterlassen können.

A   Antworten Sie: „Ja, gerne."

B   Sagen Sie, Colin sollte Sie vor 21.00 Uhr anrufen. Sagen Sie, dass es sehr wichtig ist.

A   Sagen Sie, dass Sie es ihm sofort mitteilen werden, wenn er zurückkommt. Fragen Sie B nach ihrer Telefonnummer.

B   Nennen Sie Ihre Telefonnummer. Bedanken und verabschieden Sie sich.

A   Verabschieden Sie sich.

Making Telephone Calls

Piece It Together 1

(On the phone)

A   Good morning. Rema Service.

B   Good morning. Can I have extension 236, please?

A   Just a minute. Putting you through now.

B   Thank you.

C   Paul Carter.

B   Good morning, Mr Carter. My name is Anne Scott. You tried to reach me yesterday.

C   That's right. I just wanted to make an appointment with you, to talk about next week's meeting.

B   Yes, of course. When would it suit you?

C   What about Thursday afternoon?

B   Thursday is OK with me. What time?

C   Let's say 1.45 at Rema's information desk.

B   That would suit me perfectly.

C   Fine. That's settled then.

B   All right. See you on Thursday.

C   See you. Bye!

B   Bye!

Making Telephone Calls

Role Cards (Piece It Together 1)

Good morning. Rema Service.	Good morning. Can I have extension 236, please?
Just a minute. Putting you through now.	Thank you.
Paul Carter.	Good morning, Mr Carter. My name is Anne Scott. You tried to reach me yesterday.
That's right. I just wanted to make an appointment with you, to talk about next week's meeting.	Yes, of course. When would it suit you?
What about Thursday afternoon?	Thursday is OK with me. What time?
Let's say 1.45 at Rema's information desk.	That would suit me perfectly.
Fine. That's settled then.	All right. See you on Thursday.
See you. Bye!	Bye!

Making Telephone Calls

Piece It Together 2

A 23 50 18.

B Can I speak to Mr Brown, please?

A There's no Mr Brown here. My name is Stevens. You must have got the wrong number.

B I'm awfully sorry!

A That's OK. Bye.

B Bye.

C Brown 22 50 18.

B Can I speak to Mr Brown, please?

C I'm afraid he's not in at the moment.

B Do you know when he'll be back?

C I couldn't say for sure. I could take your number and ask him to call you back, Mr …

B Dickson. James Dickson. I'm calling about the advertisement.

C Oh, I see! I'll tell him. What's your number?

B It's 31 56 77, in Brighton.

C 31 56 77. All right, Mr Dickson. I'm sure he won't be long.

B Thank you. Goodbye.

C Bye.

Making Telephone Calls

Role Cards (Piece It Together 2)

23 50 18.	Can I speak to Mr Brown, please?
There's no Mr Brown here. My name is Stevens. You must have got the wrong number.	I'm awfully sorry!
That's OK. Bye.	Bye.
Brown 22 50 18.	Can I speak to Mr Brown, please?
I'm afraid he's not in at the moment.	Do you know when he'll be back?
I couldn't say for sure. I could take your number and ask him to call you back, Mr …	Dickson. James Dickson. I'm calling about the advertisement.
Oh, I see! I'll tell him. What's your number?	It's 31 56 77, in Brighton.
31 56 77. All right, Mr Dickson. I'm sure he won't be long.	Thank you. Goodbye.
Bye.	—

YOUTH PUB

Samstag 6. Januar
Open House

ab 20 Uhr

Music, Fun, Talk, Snack

Special:

Gäste aus Costa Rica, England, Irland, Kanada, Ukraine und USA;

RC./ Dr. Külz-Str. 21: gegenüber Wohnheim Ingenieurschule

Making Telephone Calls

Piece It Together 3

(The phone is ringing.)

A   Good morning. Top Fashion.

B   Good morning. I'd like to speak to Mrs Wright, please.

A   Speaking.

B   Oh, hello! My name is Liz Parker. I had a letter from you yesterday, saying you wanted me to call you.

A   Yes, that's right. You've applied for a job at our company and I'd like you to come here for an interview.

B   Yes, of course. When would you like me to come?

A   What about 9.30 tomorrow morning?

B   Oh, dear, I'm not free then, I'm afraid.

A   Would Friday afternoon suit you better?

B   Yes, it would. What time?

A   2 o'clock?

B   Yes, that'll be fine.

A   Good! I look forward to meeting you.

B   I look forward to meeting you too!

A   See you on Friday then. Bye.

B   Bye.

Making Telephone Calls

Role Cards (Piece It Together 3)

Good morning. Top Fashion.	Good morning. I'd like to speak to Mrs Wright, please.
Speaking.	Oh, hello! My name is Liz Parker. I had a letter from you yesterday, saying you wanted me to call you.
Yes, that's right. You've applied for a job at our company and I'd like you to come here for an interview.	Yes, of course. When would you like me to come?
What about 9.30 tomorrow morning?	Oh, dear, I'm not free then, I'm afraid.
Would Friday afternoon suit you	Yes, it would. What time?
2 o'clock?	Yes, that'll be fine.
Good! I look forward to meeting you.	I look forward to meeting you too!
See you on Friday then. Bye.	Bye.

Making Telephone Calls

Role Cards (For the Teacher)

A1) Rufen Sie eine FreundIn an, um sich mit ihr zu unterhalten.

A2) Sagen Sie der AnruferIn, dass sie sich verwählt hat.

B1) Sie fragen nach jemandem. Es ist sehr wichtig.

B2) X ist den ganzen Tag nicht zu Hause.

C1) Sie können nicht zur vereinbarten Zeit kommen.
Sie rufen an, um eine andere Zeit zu vereinbaren.

C2) Versuchen Sie, einen neuen Zeitpunkt zu fixieren.

D1) Sie rufen an, weil Sie sich mit D2 an einem Abend treffen wollen.

D2) Sie haben nur am Sonntagabend und am Mittwochabend Zeit.

E1) Rufen Sie an, um etwas zu bestellen.

E2) Diese Ware ist momentan ausverkauft, ist aber nächste Woche wieder lieferbar.

F1) Jemand hat Sie gesucht. Rufen Sie an, um zu erfahren, was sie wollte.

F2) Erklären Sie F1, warum Sie sie angerufen haben.

G1) Sie wollen telefonisch Eintrittskarten für eine Veranstaltung bestellen.

G2) Die Eintrittskarten sind leider ausverkauft, aber eventuell zurückgegebene Karten können eine halbe Stunde vor Veranstaltungsbeginn am Eingang gekauft werden.

H1) Sie rufen an, um möglichst umfassende Informationen über eine bestimmte Ware zu erhalten.

H2) Antworten Sie so ausführlich wie möglich auf die Fragen.

Making Telephone Calls

Role Cards (For the Pupils)

Rufen Sie eine FreundIn an, um sich mit ihr zu unterhalten. (A 1)	Sagen Sie der AnruferIn, dass sie sich verwählt hat. (A2)
Sie fragen nach jemandem. Es ist sehr wichtig. (B1)	X ist den ganzen Tag nicht zu Hause. (B2)
Sie können nicht zur vereinbarten Zeit kommen. Sie rufen an, um eine andere Zeit zu vereinbaren. (C1)	Versuchen Sie, einen neuen Zeitpunkt zu fixieren. (C2)

Making Telephone Calls

Role Cards (For the Pupils)

Sie rufen an, weil Sie sich mit D2 an einem Abend treffen wollen. (D1)	Sie haben nur am Sonntagabend und am Mittwochabend Zeit. (D2)
Rufen Sie an, um etwas zu bestellen. (E1)	Diese Ware ist momentan ausverkauft, ist aber nächste Woche wieder lieferbar. (E2)
Jemand hat Sie gesucht. Rufen Sie an um zu erfahren, was sie wollte. (F1)	Erklären Sie F1, warum Sie sie angerufen haben. (F2)

Making Telephone Calls

Role Cards (For the Pupils)

Sie wollen telefonisch Eintrittskarten für eine Veranstaltung bestellen. (G1)	Die Eintrittskarten sind leider ausverkauft, aber eventuell zurückgegebene Karten können eine halbe Stunde vor Veranstaltungsbeginn am Eingang gekauft werden. (G2)
Sie rufen an, um möglichst umfassende Informationen über eine bestimmte Ware zu erhalten. (H1)	Antworten Sie so ausführlich wie möglich auf die Fragen. (H2)

Making Telephone Calls

Role Cards (For the Teacher)

A 1) Call a friend.

A 2) Tell the person on the phone that he/she must have got the wrong number.

B 1) You want to talk to someone. It's very important.

B 2) X isn't there today.

C 1) You can no longer come as arranged. You're calling to change the meeting.

C 2) Try and agree on a new time when you can meet.

D 1) Call to make a date with D 2.

D 2) You're only free on Wednesday evenings and Sunday evenings.

E 1) Call to order something.

E 2) You've run out of it, but it will be available again next week.

F 1) Someone's called you. Call back to find out why.

F 2) Tell F1 what you wanted.

G 1) You're calling in order to buy tickets for some event.

G 2) Tell G1 that you've sold out. Tickets which are returned will be sold at the entrance half an hour before it begins.

H 1) Call to find out as much as possible about an article.

H 2) Answer H1's questions as accurately as possible.

Making Telephone Calls

Role Cards (For the Pupils)

Call a friend. (A1)	Tell the person on the phone that he/she must have got the wrong number. (A2)
You want to talk to someone. It's very important. (B1)	X isn't there today. (B2)

Making Telephone Calls

Role Cards (For the Pupils)

You can no longer come as arranged. You're calling to change the meeting. (C 1)	Try and agree on a new time when you can meet. (C 2)
Call to make a date with D 2. (D 1)	You're only free on Wednesday evenings and Sunday evenings. (D 2)
Call to order something. (E 1)	You've run out of it, but it will be available again next week. (E 2)

Making Telephone Calls

Role Cards (For the Pupils)

Someone's called you. Call back to find out why. (F1)	Tell F1 what you wanted. (F2)
You're calling in order to buy tickets for some event. (G1)	Tell G1 that you've sold out. Tickets which are returned will be sold at the entrance half an hour before it begins. (G2)
Call to find out as much as possible about an article. (H1)	Answer H1's questions as accurately as possible. (H2)

Making Telephone Calls

Test Paper

Express yourself in good English.

(Das Telefon läutet.)

A   Melden Sie sich mit Ihrer Telefonnummer.

B   Stellen Sie sich vor und bitten Sie, mit Colin Baxter sprechen zu können.

A   Sagen Sie, B müsste sich verwählt haben.

B   Entschuldigen und verabschieden Sie sich.

A   Verabschieden Sie sich.

(Das Telefon läutet.)

C   Melden Sie sich mit „Guten Tag" und dem Namen der Firma (Porter's Garage).

B   Stellen Sie sich vor und fragen Sie, ob Colin Baxter da ist.

C   Sagen Sie, dass Sie nicht sicher sind, aber nachsehen werden.

Making Telephone Calls

C Sagen Sie, dass er gerade weggegangen ist und in ca. einer halben Stunde zurückkommen wird.

B Fragen Sie, ob Sie eine Nachricht für ihn hinterlassen können.

C Sagen Sie, dass das möglich ist.

B Bitten Sie C, Colin zu bestellen, dass er Sie so bald wie möglich anrufen soll.

C Antworten Sie: „Ja, gerne", und fragen Sie nach der Telefonnummer von B.

B Nennen Sie Ihre Nummer.

C Wiederholen Sie die Nummer und sagen Sie, dass Sie Colin informieren werden, sobald er zurückkommt.

B Bedanken und verabschieden Sie sich.

C Verabschieden Sie sich.

Lösungen

At the Tourist Office

A Excuse me, do you know where the tourist office is, please? / Excuse me, how do I get to the tourist office? / Excuse me, could you tell me the way to the tourist office, please?

B Go/Walk straight on/ahead to the first set of traffic lights. Turn right and go/carry on until you come to a park. Go/Walk through the park. The tourist office is next to/beside the church.

A Can/Could you show me on the map, please?

B Yes, of course. / Yes, certainly. It's not (very) far.

A Thank you (very much). / Thanks.

—

A Are there any places of particular interest nearby? / Are there any interesting places nearby?

C You can go to Land's End, St. Ives or Penzance.

A How much is a guided tour/a sightseeing tour to St. Ives?

C £… Lunch is included in the price. / £… including lunch.

A Can I go tomorrow? / Is there a tour/trip tomorrow? / Would it be possible to go tomorrow?

C Yes, you can. / Yes, there is. / Yes, certainly. The coach leaves at 9 am/ 9 o'clock/9 in the morning.

A Can/Could I have three tickets, please? / I'd like three tickets, please.

C That'll be £… Here you are, your tickets and a free leaflet on St. Ives. / Here are your tickets and a leaflet on St. Ives, it's free.

A Thank you (very much). / Thanks. Goodbye. / Bye.

C Goodbye. / Bye.

At the Bank

A Hello. / Good morning. / Good afternoon.

   I'd like to cash/change some traveller's cheques, please. / Can I cash traveller's cheques here?

B Certainly. / Of course. / Yes, you can. How much are they for? / How much for?

A £….

B Do you have any proof of identity? / Do you have an identity card or a passport?

A I've got my passport.

B May/Can I see it, please? / May/Can I have a look at it, please?

A Here you are.

B Please write the place and date at the top and countersign down there. / Can/Could you write the place and date here and countersign at the bottom, please?

A Here you are. / Here are the cheques.

B How would you like the money?

A I would like… (fives/tens), please. / … (fives/tens), please.

B Here's your money and your passport.

A Thank you (very much). / Thanks. Goodbye. / Bye.

B Goodbye. / Bye.

At the Post Office

A Hello. / Good morning. / Good afternoon.

B Hello. / Good morning. / Good afternoon.
   Can I help you? / What can I do for you?

A I'd like to/I want to send some letters and postcards.

B Where to? / Which country, please?

A (I've got) two letters to/for Austria, one to/for Spain and three postcards to/for Germany.

B 1st/first or 2nd/second class?

A How long will it take? / How long does it take?

B 1st class takes three days and 2nd class about a week.

A Can/Could I have six 1st class stamps, please?

B Here you are. / Here are your stamps. That'll be £…/…p

A Here's a five-pound-note/ten-pound-note. / Here's £5/£10.
(I'm afraid I don't have any change. / I'm afraid I don't have anything smaller.)

B Here's your change. £…/…p

A Thank you (very much). / Thanks. Where's the nearest letter box? / Can/Could you tell me where the nearest letter box is, please?

B It's over there in the corner.

A Thank you (very much). / Thanks. Goodbye. / Bye.

B Goodbye. / Bye.

Shopping

A Can/Could/May I try this jacket on, please? / I'd like to try this jacket on, please.

B Yes, of course. / Certainly.

A Where's the fitting room?

B It's over there.
—

A Have you got/Do you have a smaller one? / Does it come in a smaller size?

B Yes, we do. / Yes, it does.

A I (quite) like it. / I think it's nice. / It's nice. How much is it?

B It's £155.

A It's a bit expensive/That's expensive, but I'll take it anyway.

B Would you like/Do you want a carrier bag?

A No, thank you. / No, thanks.
I'd like to put it on straight away. / I'd like to wear it now.

B (Would you like) anything else?

A No, thank you. / No, thanks.

B How would you like to pay? (By) cheque, (with a) credit card or (in) cash? / What would you prefer, to pay by cheque, with a credit card or in cash?

A In cash, please. / I'd like to pay (in) cash, please.

B That's fine. / That's OK. That'll be £155, please.

A Here's £… / Here you are, £…

B Thank you (very much). / Thanks. Goodbye. / Bye.

A Goodbye. / Bye.

Eating Out

A Can/Could/May I have the menu, please? / I'd like to see the menu, please.

B Here you are (, Sir/Madam).
—

B Can I take your order (, Sir/Madam)? / Are you ready to order (, Sir/Madam)?

A Yes, I'd like a starter, please. (I'll have)…

B Would you like a main course? / Would you like anything to follow?

A Yes, please.
I'd like… , please. / I'll have… , please.

B Would you like a sweet/dessert as well?

A No, thank you/thanks, but I'd like/love something to drink.

B We have… / You can have…

A I'd like…
—

A Can/Could/May I have the bill, please? / I'd like the bill, please.

B Here you are. / Here's your bill. That'll be £…

A Is service included? / Is that including service?

B Yes, it is.

A Here's £… / Here you are, £…

B Thank you (, Sir/Madam). We hope to see you again.

A Thank you (very much) / Thanks. Goodbye. / Bye.

B Goodbye. / Bye.

Being Ill

A Hello. / Good morning. / Good afternoon.

B Hello. / Good morning. / Good afternoon.
Can I help you? / What can I do for you?

A I'm not feeling (very) well. / I feel unwell.

B What's wrong with you? / What seems to be the trouble? / What's the matter/problem?

A I think I've got/caught a cold.

B Have you been to the doctor? / Have you seen a doctor? / Have you been to see your doctor?

A I didn't think it was necessary.
I've only got a headache and a sore throat.

B Why don't you get yourself some throat lozenges and a bottle of aspirin? / I suggest you buy some throat lozenges and a bottle of aspirin. / Buy some throat lozenges and a bottle of aspirin. You won't/don't need a prescription for those.

A That sounds/seems like a good idea. / That sounds good.
How much are they?

B £… / That'll be £…

A Here's £… / Here you are, £…

B Here's your change and your medicine.

A Thank you (very much). / Thanks. Goodbye. / Bye.

B Goodbye. / Bye.

At the Railway Station

A Excuse me, do you know where the ticket office is, please? / Excuse me, do you know where I can buy tickets? / Excuse me, where's the ticket office?

B It's/The ticket office is opposite the waiting room.

A Thank you (very much). / Thanks.

—

A Hello. / Good morning. / Good afternoon.
Can/Could/May I have a ticket to London, please? / I'd like a ticket to London, please.

C Single or return? / Do you want a single or a return ticket?

A Return, please. / I'd like a return ticket, please.

C Are you coming back today? / Will you be coming back today?

A Yes, tonight. / Yes, this evening.

C Why don't you buy a cheap day return ticket? / I suggest you buy a cheap day return ticket.

A How much is it?

C £… / It's £…

A When is the next train to London?

C There's one in (about) … minutes. / It leaves at …

A How long does it take?
Do I have to change (trains)?

C (It takes) about an hour, it's a through train/an express train.
You won't/don't have to change (trains).

A Which platform does it leave from?

C Platform … / It/Your train leaves from platform …

A Thank you (very much). / Thanks. Goodbye. / Bye.

C Thank you. Have a nice journey.

Making Telephone Calls

A … (z. B. 28 17 60).

B (Hello. / Good morning. / Good afternoon.) This is … /
My name is …
Can/Could/May I speak to Colin Baxter, please? / I'd like to speak to Colin Baxter, please.

A I'm afraid you must have dialled the wrong number. / I'm afraid you've got the wrong number.

B (Oh!) I'm (awfully/terribly) sorry. Goodbye. / Bye.

A Goodbye. / Bye.

—

C Good afternoon. Porter's Garage.

147

B This is … / My name is …
  Is Colin Baxter in/there?

C I'm not sure. / I don't (really) know.
  I'll have a look. / I'll see if he's in/here.

C He's just gone out. He'll be back in
  about half an hour/30 minutes.

B Can/May I leave a message? /
  Can/Could you give him a message?

C Certainly. / Yes, of course.

B Can/Could you ask Colin/him to call
  me back as soon as possible? / Please tell
  him to call me back as soon as possible.

C Yes. / Certainly. / Of course.
  What's your number? / Could/Can/May
  I have your number, please? / What
  number are you calling from?

B My number is …

C … I'll let him know when he comes
  back. / I'll give him the/your message
  when he comes back.

B Thank you (very much). / Thanks.
  Goodbye. / Bye.

C Goodbye. / Bye.